CHAPTERS FROM A FLOATING LIFE

THE AUTOBIOGRAPHY OF
A CHINESE ARTIST

CHAPTERS
FROM A FLOATING LIFE

THE AUTOBIOGRAPHY OF A CHINESE ARTIST

SHEN FU

Translated from the Chinese by
SHIRLEY M. BLACK

Poems by Tu Fu and Li Po
Translated by S. M. B.

LONDON
OXFORD UNIVERSITY PRESS
NEW YORK, TORONTO
1960

Oxford University Press, Amen House, London E.C.4

GLASGOW   NEW YORK   TORONTO   MELBOURNE   WELLINGTON
BOMBAY   CALCUTTA   MADRAS   KARACHI   KUALA LUMPUR
CAPE TOWN   IBADAN   NAIROBI   ACCRA

B
S

erl

PRINTED IN GREAT BRITAIN

FOR BOB

CONTENTS

LIST OF ILLUSTRATIONS

INTRODUCTION

SHEN FU, whose memoirs I have translated as *Chapters from a Floating Life*, was a painter and writer of Soochow in Kiangsu, a region of China long famous for the beauty of its women and the genius of its artists. Shen Fu was a failure—sensitive, romantic and impractical; a lover of beauty and laughter, of flowers and wine, of the wonders of nature and the company of good friends. His poet wife, Ch'en Yün, was a literate individualist. Charming, talented and gay, too independent of mind to fit easily into the household of her young husband's family, she inevitably aroused the suspicion and antagonism of mean souls.

The two artists early found themselves as much out of place in the life of conservative Chinese officialdom as would a similar couple in the political or commercial environment of our twentieth century. The problems faced by Shen Fu and Yün, and the pressures which ultimately destroyed them, were essentially the same problems and pressures which have confronted and destroyed the gentle, beauty-loving nonconformists at almost all times and in almost all places. Man has seldom been tolerant of the eccentric in his midst. But Shen Fu—dogged by misfortune, harassed by creditors, existing in miserable poverty as he did—yet managed to leave in his memoirs one of the tenderest and happiest of all love stories.

Eldest son of a scholar family, Shen Fu was apprenticed to his father's profession, that of secretary to magistrates, and in 1786 was appointed to his first post with the magistrate at Chi-hsi in Anhwei. Resigning a year later, following a disagreement with a fellow secretary, he joined a relative in the brewing business, only to have a rebellion in Formosa ruin their trade with that island; and as this trade was the backbone of the enterprise, the business failed. After this Shen Fu worked sporadically as secretary, teacher and merchant, but never held any post for very long. In 1803, while they were living in miserable circumstances in Yangchow, his wife Yün died. His father's death followed a year later.

Cheated out of his inheritance through the machinations of his younger brother, Shen Fu was then reduced to living for a time on the charity of friends in Soochow, until, in 1805, he went to Chung-king as secretary to his old friend, Shih Yün-yü. In 1806 he found a post with the magistrate at Lai-yang in Shantung, but left shortly after to accompany his friend, Shih Yün-yü, to Peking. From that city he went the following year as secretary with an embassy to the Loochoo Islands, where he spent several years. After 1807 we know nothing of Shen Fu's life, though it is known that he acquired some fame as a painter after his return from the islands, and that he painted a scroll on the subject of his voyage to Loochoo, for which Shih Yün-yü wrote a colophon.

Shen Fu's autobiography, the title of which can be literally translated as *Six Memoirs of a Floating Life*, is a literary masterpiece; poetic, romantic, nostalgic and filled with emotion, it recreates a life essentially tragic, which yet held innumerable moments of an almost magical happiness and beauty. The work was originally in six sections, but when the manuscript turned up in a second-hand bookstore in Soochow in 1877 the last two sections were missing. The four remaining parts were first printed in that same year and have since been reprinted many times. The book is still widely read and can be bought today in any Chinese bookstore. An edition containing six parts was published in 1935, but the last two parts were obviously not authentic, being reprints from the works of various well-known authors. The edition I used was published within the last few years by the Wu Kuei T'ang (Five Cassia Hall) Publishing Company of Hong Kong. It too contains the spurious sections, neither of which I have included in this translation.

In translating the memoirs I have tried first of all to recreate the subtle emotional atmosphere, at once tragic, passionate and gay, which is, in my opinion, the outstanding characteristic of Shen Fu's original. I have also tried to be as meticulous as I could in expressing the exact meaning of the Chinese words, at the same time trying to approximate the feeling of the author's own way of expressing himself. This is a rather difficult job with languages as different from one another as Chinese and English and I do not know that I have even partially succeeded.

Each of the six parts of the memoirs deals with a different aspect of the author's life; the first with his marriage; the second with small satisfactions and pleasures like gardening, flower arranging and the decoration of houses; the third with the misfortunes that plagued his entire existence, and the fourth with an account of his travels to Canton and other places of scenic interest. The lost parts recounted in one his voyage to the Loochoo Islands and in the other, the experiences of his later years and his ideas on life and living.

I have omitted many episodes from the fourth part, concerned with visits to temples and scenic places, which are rather alike and would not mean much to the reader unacquainted with the actual places described. Some sections of literary criticism, gardening and botany I have also left out, as I felt they were of too specialized a nature to be of general interest. Other episodes I have rearranged into a less confusing chronological order.

The Wade system of transliteration was used in spelling all the names except Yün's, which I have spelled Yuen, thinking that this spelling would give a somewhat better approximation of the Chinese pronunciation.

The illustrations used in the book are reproductions of paintings by some of the best of the individualist painters of the Ch'ing dynasty—paintings which Shen Fu, Yün and their friends might have chosen, and in styles in which they might well have painted.

I should like to thank my friends Martha and LeRoy Davidson for their suggestion that I use such paintings as illustrations for the book. I should also like to thank the museum officials who made it possible for me to use the paintings from their galleries: Laurence Sickman, Director of the William Rockhill Nelson Gallery of Art, Kansas City; and James F. Cahill of the Freer Gallery of Art, Washington, D.C.

Claremont, 1959   SHIRLEY M. BLACK

'In this dream-like, floating life
how often are we happy?'

From a poem by L I P O

PART ONE

CHAPTER 1

I WAS born in 1763, at a time of peace and unusual prosperity, in the reign of the Emperor Ch'ien Lung, on the twenty-second day of the eleventh month, in the winter of the year of the sheep. Mine was a full-dress family, one of scholars and gentle-people, who lived near the gardens of the Ts'ang-lang Pavilion, in the city of Soochow.

The gods, I should say, have always been more than generous to me; but, as the poet Su Tung-p'o wrote:

> 'Life is like a spring dream
> which ends—and leaves no traces.'

By setting down this story of my life, then, I hope to show my gratitude for Heaven's many favours.

The first of the three hundred poems in the *Classic of Poetry* is a wedding song and I too shall begin with memories of my married life, letting other events follow as they may. My only regret is that as a boy I neglected my studies and acquired such a superficial education that now I find it impossible to do more than record the bare facts of my life as I remember them. Examining my work for elegance of style, therefore, would be like expecting brilliance from a tarnished mirror.

I remember that when I was a small boy I could stare into the sun with wide-open eyes. I remember, too, that I could see very clearly such minute autumn hairs as the down on plants and the markings on the tiniest insects. I loved to look closely at anything delicate or small; examining the grains of pieces of wood, the veins and patterns of leaves or the streaks and lines on some insignificant trifle, gave me an almost magical delight.

In summer when the mosquitoes were buzzing like thunder, I used to pretend they were a company of cranes dancing in the air. My imagination transformed them into real birds, into hundreds and thousands of actual cranes; and I would keep my eyes on them, entranced, until I had a crick in my neck from looking upwards so intently. Once I trapped some mosquitoes behind a thin white curtain and carefully blew smoke around them until their humming became the crying of the cranes and I could see the white birds flying through the azure clouds of highest heaven. How happy I was at that moment!

I often used to crouch in the hollow of a ruined wall or squat on my heels beside one of the raised flower terraces, my eyes on a level with the plants and grasses, and with rapt attention stare at some minute object until, in my mind, I had transformed the grass into a dense forest and the insects and ants into wild beasts. With my spirit wandering happily in this world of my imagination I would then see the small stones as towering mountains, the slight depressions in the earth as deep ravines.

One day, as I watched two insects fighting in the grass, a huge and terrible monster burst upon the scene, toppling the mountains and flattening the trees as it came. Suddenly, I saw it swallow the fighting insects with one flick of its enormous tongue! And so far away was my childish spirit at that moment that I failed to recognize the monster as just an ordinary toad. I opened my mouth and screamed with terror. When I finally came to my senses, seeing then that it was nothing but a toad,

I picked the animal up, beat it several tens of times and chased it off the terrace.

Years later, in thinking of this incident, I realized that the two insects had not been fighting but that I had been witness to an act of rape. The ancient proverb says: 'Destruction follows fornication.' This would seem to apply to insects also!

Another time, while I was enjoying a secret pleasure in the garden, my egg (we call the male organ an 'egg' in Soochow slang), was nipped by an earthworm and soon became so badly swollen that I could not urinate. After a duck had been caught for the purpose, a servant was told to hold the animal so that the saliva from its open mouth would drip onto my swollen egg. When the girl carelessly loosened her grip on its neck for a moment, the duck tried to swallow my egg, and I—scared out of my senses—set up a tremendous hullabaloo. Tongues wagged over all this, you may be sure.

Such were the idle pastimes of my childhood.

When I was still a small boy I became engaged to a daughter of the Yu family of Chin-sha; but, as the little girl died before her eighth birthday, I eventually married one of my cousins, the daughter of my mother's brother Ch'en Hsin-yu. My wife's intimate name was Yuen, meaning Fragrant Herb. Her literary name, by which we often called her, was Shu-chen, Precious Virtue.

Even as a baby Yuen had shown signs of unusual intelligence and understanding. Not long after she had learned to talk her parents taught her to recite Po Chu-i's long narrative poem 'The Song of the Lute'. After hearing it once or twice, the child could repeat the whole poem from beginning to end, word for word, without making a single mistake.

Yuen's father died when she was four years old, leaving his family—wife, son, and daughter—with nothing but the four bare walls of an empty house. But as she grew up the girl became a skilful needlewoman, able to fill three mouths from the work of her ten clever fingers, and to pay the school fees for her brother, K'e-chang, when he commenced to study with a tutor.

One day, in a waste-paper basket, Yuen found a copy of *The Song of the Lute*. From the tattered pages of the discarded book, with her memory of the words of the poem to guide her, she learned to recognize the characters and in this way taught herself to read. Stealing moments now and then from her embroidery, she not only learned to read poetry but soon began writing verses herself. I have always particularly liked these two lines from one of her early poems:

> 'Invaded by autumn, men are lean as shadows;
> Fattening on frost, chrysanthemums grow lush.'

When I was thirteen I went with my mother to visit the home of her parents and there I met my cousin Yuen for the first time. Two equally ingenuous children, we were drawn to each other at once. Yuen trusted me enough, from the beginning, to show me the poems she had written. Reading them, I realized that hers was a very unusual talent, but the knowledge made me afraid that, in this world, such a clever girl would be neither happy nor fortunate.

After I returned to my own home, finding that I could not put my cousin out of my mind or my heart, I decided to talk to my mother about her.

'In case you are thinking of choosing a wife for me soon,' I said, 'I must tell you that I cannot marry anyone but my cousin Shu-chen.'

Fortunately for me, my mother had also grown fond of her niece. Yuen's grace and beauty and the gentleness of her manner had so pleased my mother that she now took off her own gold wedding-ring and decided to send it to my cousin as a token of our engagement. This took place in 1775, on the sixteenth day of the seventh month of the year of the sheep.

Some months later, in the winter of that same year, when one of my girl cousins was about to be married, I once again accompanied my mother to her family home for the wedding celebrations.

Now that we were together again, Yuen and I continued to call one another 'Younger Brother' and 'Elder Sister Precious', just as we had done before, although my cousin was only ten months my elder.

The house was gay, on this ceremonious occasion, with the rainbow-hued new robes of the family and the wedding guests. Yuen alone, looked her quiet, simple self, having added nothing to her everyday dress but a pair of bright new shoes. When I had admired the artistry of their embroidery and learned that she had made the shoes herself, I began to understand that Yuen was extremely capable and practical; that reading, writing, and composing poetry were only a few of her many accomplishments.

The simplicity of her robe seemed to accentuate her fragile beauty and the slenderness of her graceful figure, with its sloping shoulders and long, delicate neck. Her eyes looked very dark beneath the curving wings of her brows. Her glance sparkled with intelligence and humour, and I could find no flaw in her loveliness except that her two front teeth sloped forward ever so slightly under short upper lip; an unimportant defect, but one that was regarded as a sign of bad luck. Above all else, a clinging softness in her manner, an indefinable air of tenderness and vulnerability about her, touched my heart deeply, making me wish to stay forever by her side.

I had asked Yuen to let me read the rough drafts of her latest poems, but found, when she gave me the manuscript, that most of the verses were unfinished, being couplets, or at most, stanzas of only three or four lines.

'Why do you never finish them, Sister Shu?' I asked her.

'Without a teacher, I have never learned to finish them

5

correctly,' she answered. 'I wish I had an intimate friend who would also be my teacher and help me with my poetry.'

Taking the book of poems from her hand I playfully wrote on the label:

'Beautiful Lines in a Brocade Cover.'

I could not know, then, that hidden within those covers were the reasons for her early death!

That evening I formally escorted the bridal party to a celebration outside the city walls and before I reached home again the watchman at the water-clock had called the third watch of the night. I was feeling very hungry. Entering the house, I called a servant and asked her to bring me some meat dumplings, but the old woman came back with some dates and dried meats from the wedding feast, sweets which I do not like and will not eat.

Yuen heard my voice. She came out and pulled me by the sleeve, motioning me to follow her to her room, where I was delighted to find that she had hidden some rice-gruel and vegetables for my supper. I was raising the chop-sticks to my mouth, when I heard Yuen's cousin, Yu-heng, calling:

'Sister Shu. Sister Shu. Come quickly.' Yuen rose at once and shut the door.

'I'm very tired,' she called to Yu-heng. 'I was just going to bed.'

Yu-heng pushed hard against the door and managed to squeeze into the room. When he saw me, chop-sticks in air, he grinned at Yuen and laughed maliciously.

'A little while ago I asked you to bring me some congee,' he said, 'but you told me it was all gone. But now I see that you were saving it to serve to your husband!'

Tearful and embarrassed, Yuen looked as if she wanted to run away and hide. A crowd of relatives and servants, attracted by Yu-heng's noisy laughter, began crowding into the room, joining in the fun at Yuen's expense. I too became very excited and upset. I called my personal servant and left for my own home at once, in a very bad humour. After this distressing incident, Yuen tried to avoid me whenever I visited her home, but I understood that she was keeping out of my way because she dreaded being ridiculed again on my account.

CHAPTER 2

FIVE years were to pass before our wedding candles burned, at dusk, on the twenty-second day of the first month of the year of the rat—1780. As Yuen stepped from her bridal chair I saw at once that she had not changed, that hers was still the same delicate, sensitive figure I knew so well in my dreams. When, at last, she raised the wedding veil which had hidden her face, we looked at one another long and steadily; then Yuen smiled at me—and I found her as enchanting as before.

After drinking together from the ceremonial nuptial cup, we took our places side by side at the wedding banquet. I felt for Yuen's wrist, under the table, then closed my hand over her slender fingers. The touch of her smooth skin, so warm and soft, made my head swim and my heart beat violently.

I begged her to begin eating but she whispered that she was keeping a vegetarian fast, and had eaten no meat for several years. When I questioned her, she told me shyly that she had begun her secret fast at the time when I had smallpox.

'But Sister Shu,' I said teasingly, 'now that my face is clear and smooth again, without a single scar, won't you please break your fast?' Yuen's eyes smiled into mine as she nodded her head.

One of my sisters was to be married on the twenty-fourth, but, as the twenty-third was a day of national mourning when

7

no music could be played, her wedding banquet, also, took place on my wedding night. While Yuen watched my sister's entertainment in the banquet hall I was playing the guess-fingers game with the bride's attendant in my bridal chamber.

As penalty for shouting a wrong number in this fast guessing game, the loser is required to drink a cup of wine. Being con-sistently defeated, drinking cup after cup of wine, I was soon so very drunk that I collapsed on the floor in a stupor. Before I was sober enough to open my eyes again, my wedding night had passed; dawn was whitening the window and Yuen was nearly dressed.

We spent the long day entertaining relatives and friends, who kept coming and going, in a continuous stream, until after the lamps had been lighted and the musicians were again permitted to play. Soon after midnight, on the morning of the twenty-fourth, in my ceremonial capacity as brother of the bride, I formally escorted my sister to her new husband's home. Returning about three o'clock, I found the courtyards deserted and silent. The last guest had gone home. The last candles were flickering out.

Quietly, I entered my bridal chamber, where the bride's attendant lay dozing on the floor. Yuen, who had taken off her wedding finery, was not yet in bed. She was sitting, in the light from a pair of tall silver candles, with her delicate white neck bent over a book, so completely absorbed in her reading that she was unaware I had come into the room.

I put my hand on her shoulder.

'The past few days have been tiring and difficult for you, Sister,' I said. 'Why are you still reading? Aren't you worn out?'

Quickly raising her head, Yuen rose respectfully to her feet.

'I was ready to go to bed when I went to the cupboard and picked out this book,' she explained. 'As soon as I started to read it I forgot how exhausted I was. For years I have been hearing about *The West Chamber*, but this is the first time I have ever really seen a copy. The author was certainly a genius—though I find his style a little too biting, too satirical.'

'But only a writer who is really a genius can write good satire,' I answered.

The bride's attendant interrupted, yawning, to suggest that it was time we went to bed. When I told her to leave us, she went out and closed the door behind her. Left alone for the first time, Yuen and I stood side by side, laughing softly, feeling as excited as two old friends who meet again after a long separation. Playfully, I put my hand on her breast and felt the wild beating of her heart. Bending close, I whispered softly,

'Shu-chen, why does your heart beat like this?' Yuen's eyes smiled into mine, and in that moment our souls were closely bound with the silken strands of love; our quivering bodies knew the intensity of desire.

So, at last, I led her to the bed, nor were we aware when dawn began to whiten the horizon.

Though she was at first reserved and silent, Yuen, as a young bride, was never angry nor sullen. She was respectful to her elders and treated her inferiors with gentle kindness, nor could the slightest fault be found with the work she did in the household. Every morning, as the sun sent its first rays through the window, Yuen would get out of bed, hastily putting on her clothes as if she heard someone ordering her to do so.

'You are a married woman now,' I laughed at her. 'Your position is very different from the time when I ate your congee. Why are you still so afraid of being criticized?'

'When I hid the rice-gruel for you, I really did give cause for gossip,' she answered. 'Now, although I am no longer afraid at being laughed at, I don't want to give your parents any occasion to think I am lazy or careless.'

I wanted to make love to her again; to hold her in my arms a little longer; yet I had such respect for her strength of character that I made myself get out of bed as soon as she did, so that all through the day we were inseparable, heads together, as close as a man and his shadow. Words cannot describe the depth of our emotions, the joy we shared, the love and passion we felt for each other. But joy and pleasure make time fly all too swiftly and, in what seemed no more than a flutter of the eyelashes, the month of our honeymoon had passed.

My father, who was then secretary to a high official at Kuei-ch'i, now sent a yamen constable to fetch me back with him, as I was still, at that time, a pupil of the tutor Mr. Chao Sheng-chai of Wu-lin. (It is entirely due to the efforts of this Mr. Chao, a talented and conscientious teacher, that I am literate at all today.) Although I had known all along that after the wedding I should have to return to my studies, the arrival of my father's message disturbed and depressed me and my heart sank at the thought that Yuen might break into tears at the news of my going.

But Yuen, to my surprise, presented a cheerful face. She tried to encourage me in my plans and started at once to pack my boxes for the journey to Kuei-ch'i. It was not until evening that I became aware of her unnatural, set expression and realized that she was not her usual self. As I was about to leave she came close to me and whispered:

'Now you will have no one to take care of you; please try to be careful, and look after yourself.'

The hawser was cast off as soon as I boarded the boat. Along the banks of the canal the peach and plum trees were in full bloom, the sight of their fragile beauty filling my heart with loneliness and desolation. Confused as a forest bird that has lost the flock, I felt that Heaven and earth alike were menacing and strange.

Immediately after arriving at Kuei-ch'i, I had to say good-bye to my father who was about to cross the river on an official journey to an eastern part of the country. The next three months, as I dragged my way through them, felt like ten years of unendurable separation. Letters from Yuen arrived regularly enough, although for two of mine I received only one in reply; but of these, half were filled with words of caution or encouragement, the rest with mere frivolous conventionalities.

Sadness and dejection filled my heart. Every time the wind rustled the bamboos in my courtyard or the moon silvered the leaves of the banana trees beside my window, I remembered other moons and other nights until my soul became entranced with an unreal world of dreams and fancies. My tutor, becoming aware of my condition, wrote at once to my father, saying that he intended to assign me ten themes for composition before sending me back to my wife for the time being.

Happy as a pardoned prisoner of war I boarded the boat again, but now, to my sorrow, it seemed to me that time had begun to run backwards; that every quarter of an hour took a year to go by.

Reaching home at last, I hurriedly paid my respects to my mother before rushing to my own room, where Yuen waited to greet me. We clung to each other, beyond words; wildly excited, one soul in one body; dizzy with happiness in a world of mist and clouds.

It was then the sixth month; the weather was very sultry and the whole house was hot and damp. Fortunately, we were living next door to the Lotus Lover's Retreat of the Ts'ang-lang Pavilion Gardens, which lay to the west of our courtyards. Across a wooden foot-bridge, overlooking the canal, stood a small open pavilion called 'My Choice'; the allusion referring to the 'choices' in the ancient lines:

> 'If the water is clear—wash your cap strings;
> If it is muddy—wash your feet.'

Beyond the eaves of 'My Choice' an old tree raised its gnarled trunk; its branches throwing a dense shade across the windows, dyeing our faces green. People, in an endless line, passed back and forth along the opposite bank of the canal, so that my father, when he was entertaining friends in the pavilion, always lowered the blinds on that side. After asking my mother's permission, I now moved with Yuen to 'My Choice', intending to stay there for the rest of the summer.

Because of the extreme heat, Yuen had put her embroidery aside. We spent the long, hot, summer days together; doing nothing but reading, discussing the classics, enjoying the moonlight, or idly admiring the flowers.

Yuen was not used to drinking, though she could take two or three cups if she had to, and I would often amuse myself by teaching her to play various literary games in which the loser must empty a cup of wine.

In all the world, we thought, no life could be happier than this!

Yuen was very quiet in those first days at the pavilion but she soon overcame her shyness and learned to express herself clearly and with ease. One day, while resting in the shade of the ancient tree, we began exchanging ideas on the literature of classic times.

'An appreciation of classical literature,' Yuen said, 'requires a breadth of knowledge and a nobility of thought that are, I am afraid, too difficult for a woman to attain. I think, though, that I do have some slight understanding and awareness of poetry.'

'Poetry was used in the selection of scholars for official posts, in the T'ang dynasty,' I told her. 'And of all the T'ang poets, everyone agrees that Tu Fu and Li Po are the greatest masters. Which do you prefer, darling?'

'Tu Fu, I think, is first of all a master of style,' she answered. 'His work is admired as much for its refinement of form as for its grandeur of conception. Li's poems, on the other hand, are free and unconventional, filled with freshness and vigour. I admire the dignity and majesty of Master Tu,' she smiled, 'but I prefer the freedom and liveliness of Master Li'.

'Nevertheless, Tu Fu is acknowledged to be the greatest of all poets,' I argued. 'His verses are still used as models of form by most students of poetry. Listen to this poem on autumn in the gorges of the Yang-tze River.'

AUTUMN

Jade dew of autumn
pearls the grove of withered maples;
Silence and desolation brood
over mountain and gorge.
Wave after wave of the swiftly-flowing river
rises to meet the sky
as over the lofty passes
clouds race before the wind
to catch their shadows on the earth below.

Chrysanthemums grow rank,
like twice-shed tears—a second time in bloom.
Here though my lonely boat is tied
my heart looks back to its old home.
Everywhere, with scissors and measure
they hurry the winter robes
as sunset touches
the soaring walls of Po-ti
to the hurried pounding of the washing-stones.

'Since you alone prefer Li Po, my darling,' I continued, 'will you tell me why?'

'For perfection of form, beauty of phrase, and nobility of thought Tu's poems are certainly unequalled,' Yuen admitted; 'but Li's poems have the lyric charm of fairy maidens. He seems to write as naturally as petals fall and waters flow. That is why I love him.

'"Hearing the Flute on a Spring Night" has always been one of my favourites.

'Tones of a jade flute—flying from whose hidden garden—
Floating on the breeze—scattering over Lo City.

I listen in darkness to "Breaking of the Willow"—
And memories of home fill my heart.

'It is not that I consider Tu Fu inferior to Li Po,' she contined; 'I admire and appreciate Tu's poems, but I love Li Po's.'

'Who would have thought,' I laughed, 'that you were so intimate with Li Po—I did not know that you were old friends!'

Yuen smiled.

'I have still another favourite,' she said, 'Po Chü-i; my childhood teacher, you might say. In my heart I shall always be grateful to him.'

'What do you mean?' I asked.

'Isn't he the author of "The Song of the Lute"?'

'How very strange!' I laughed. 'Li Po is your bosom friend; Po Chu-i, your first teacher, and I, with the literary name of San-po (Three Po's), am your husband. Your destiny seems linked to the character "po".'

'If "po" characters are my fate,' Yuen smiled, 'I'm afraid there will always be "po" characters in my poems.' (In Soochow we call incorrectly written characters, 'po' characters.) Finding this very funny, we both burst out laughing.

I am naturally straightforward and easy-going, unhampered by convention; but Yuen, like a pedantic old Confucian scholar, firmly believed in propriety and ceremony, and insisted on observing many old-fashioned formalities in our daily life. Whenever I helped her into a robe or adjusted a sleeve for her she would murmur repeatedly, 'I'm so sorry to trouble you. I'm so sorry to trouble you.' If I brought her a handkerchief or a fan she would insist on rising to receive it from me. At first, this bored me. I disliked it and one day I mentioned it to her.

'Darling, must you entangle me in all this ceremony? You know the old saying, "He who is too polite must be deceitful".'

Cheeks on fire, Yuen replied:

'When I am trying to be properly respectful and courteous to you, isn't it ironical that you should accuse me of being deceitful?'

'Genuine respect is in the heart,' I retorted, 'not in empty formalities.'

'The closest of all relationships is that between parent and child,' Yuen countered; 'should we then respect our parents in our hearts while behaving outwardly with bad manners and lack of consideration?'

'Forget my words,' I begged her. 'I only spoke in fun.'

'Most quarrels between husbands and wives start in fun,' she answered seriously. 'Please do not be angry with me again, or I shall die of grief.'

Taking her in my arms then, I held her closely, caressing her until she looked into my eyes and smiled again. Our conversation, after this, became full of terms of politeness; of 'excuse me's', 'so sorry's', and 'I beg your pardon's'. We lived the years of our short married life with a courtesy and harmony worthy of Liang Hung and Meng Kuang, whose story is told in the *Records of the Han Dynasty*. Here is the tale as I remember it.

Meng Kuang was a lady of strong mind, renowned virtue and regrettable lack of beauty, whose family home had been located by Fortune close to that of the wise scholar Liang Hung. Still unmarried, Liang Hung declared that no woman had so far been able to satisfy his ideal of wifely virtue. Meng Kuang also had refused to marry, telling her parents that the only man for whom she had sufficient respect to consider as a husband was the eminent Liang Hung. She persisted in this course until her thirtieth year, when the scholar, learning of her steadfast attachment, decided to make her his wife.

After the wedding, he was displeased to see that his plain-featured wife had decked herself out in traditional feminine finery; but Meng Kuang, sensing that she had offended her husband, immediately changed into rough, simple clothing, and from that moment served her lord with a fitting humility and obedience. Contented and happy in her poor surroundings, she insisted on showing the respect in which she held her husband by raising the rice bowl to the level of her eyebrows whenever they sat down to a meal. Or so the story goes!

CHAPTER 3

WITH every passing day, Yuen and I grew more deeply attached to one another, more passionately in love. In the house, if we met by chance in a dark room or unexpectedly brushed sleeves in a narrow passage, our hands would cling together as we whispered quickly, 'Where are you going, darling?'; making sure that no one saw or heard us, we tried to keep our love a secret from prying eyes.

Through shyness at first, we tried to avoid being seen together at all, afraid that someone might notice us talking together or taking a walk in the garden, but soon, we began to forget our self-consciousness and were no longer concerned, eventually, with what others might think. If Yuen sat chatting with a friend and saw me coming, she would at once rise and move over, making room for me to sit down beside her, doing

石骨泉心各自靈一癡一醒
解相成多情洗出磷磷碧洗
到清時石更明

1. Chinese painting by Hua Yen, dated in correspondence
with A.D. 1729. From an album at the Freer Gallery
of Art, Washington, D.C.

2. Chinese painting by Kung Hsien (Kung Pan-chien), active about 1660–1700. From a handscroll in the William Rockhill Nelson Gallery of Art, Kansas City, Missouri.

this quite naturally and almost without thinking; though to do so would at first have made her feel ashamed, by this time it had become a matter of habit.

How strange it is that so many elderly couples seem to regard each other as enemies! I cannot understand it. I know it is a common saying that 'two people who are not enemies can never live to old age together', I still refuse to believe it.

To celebrate the festival of the Herd-boy and the Weaver-girl, on the seventh night of the seventh month, Yuen arranged some candles, incense and fruit on a table at the pavilion called 'My Choice', so that she and I could pay our respects to the Heavenly Lovers together.

The story goes that the Weaver-girl was separated from her lover, the Herd-boy, by the angry Emperor of Heaven, who wished the Weaver-girl to return to her task of weaving the garments of the Gods. But the two poor lovers mourned each other so long and so faithfully that the magpies at last took pity on them. Every year, on the seventh night of the seventh moon, if the skies are clear, the birds fly to the Milky Way, the River of Stars, there to form a bridge with their wings and bodies, over which the Heavenly Lovers pass to their yearly meeting, once again renewing their vows of eternal devotion.

I had carved two seals for this occasion, bearing the inscription: 'Grant us re-incarnation as husband and wife throughout eternity.' The intaglio, white-character seal I gave to Yuen, keeping the reverse, red-character one for myself. These seals, we decided, should be used only on our letters to one another.

Brilliant moonlight had silvered the quiet garden as I watched the shining satin ripples of the stream. The night was very hot. We were sitting before the water-window, dressed in light silk gowns, fanning ourselves languidly with little gauze fans, looking first at the water below us, then at the ever-changing shapes of the scudding clouds in the skies overhead.

'In all the wide Universe there is only one moon,' Yuen

17

C

mused. 'Do you suppose there could be another pair of lovers on this earth who love each other as much as we do?'

'Lovers like us will be everywhere tonight,' I answered; 'like us, they will be sitting in the cool breeze, enjoying the moonlight and exclaiming over the beauty of the clouds. Even girls who cannot leave the inner apartments will be drawing aside the curtains to watch the skies, and there must be many quiet scholars who will prefer to spend such an evening in solitude. But if married lovers like us are watching the moon, I do not think they will be admiring the clouds for very long!'

By now, the candles had gone out. The moon was low in the sky. Slowly we removed the dishes of fruit and went to bed.

Half a li from my home, in Vinegar Storehouse Lane, stood a temple to the Goddess of Tung-t'ing Lake, The Temple of the Water-Fairy, commonly called the Narcissus Temple. The temple itself, a maze of intricate corridors and winding verandas, was surrounded by a small, commonplace garden, with pavilions and arbours scattered here and there.

Every year, on the birthday of the goddess, each family in the neighbourhood was given its own particular spot in the temple, which the members of the clan would decorate with hanging lanterns of a special kind having shelves in the centre for holding vases of flowers. Under the lanterns, on low tables at either side, they would arrange other vases, filling them with flowers that would later be judged in a floral competition.

Theatrical performances filled the day, and at night the place was brilliantly lighted by candles placed among the vases; a custom called 'illumination of the flowers'. The colour and fragrance of the blossoms, the flickering shadows cast by the lanterns and candles, and the swirling smoke that floated above the bronze tripods of the incense-burners, all combined to create the impression of a feast by night in the Hall of the Dragon King.

The exhibiting families, to while away the hours, would play music and sing, drink tea and gossip, while the townspeople looked on, crowding like ants against the railings set up under the eaves. I was fortunate enough to be able to take an active part in the festival when some friends invited me to go with them to help arrange the candles and flowers. In the evening, when I came home to Yuen, I enthusiastically described the beauty of the scene.

'What a pity I am not a man,' she sighed; 'if I were, I could go with you and see it all for myself.'

'If you wore one of my hats and gowns,' I told her, 'I think you could easily pass for a man.' At once, she began to take down her long hair, quickly braiding it into a masculine queue. Then she thickened and darkened her beautiful moth-eyebrows with paint, before putting my hat on her head. The deception was quite successful in spite of the hair that still showed slightly around her temples. Finding, when she tried it on, that my gown was several inches too long for her, she stitched a tuck around the waist and covered it with a short jacket.

'But my feet,' she wailed, 'what can I do about them?'

Remembering that there were special shops selling 'butterfly shoes', that can be worn with either bound or natural feet, I told her I would buy her a pair:

'And you can wear them afterwards for house slippers,' I suggested.

Yuen was delighted. After supper she insisted on dressing-up again, and once more braiding her queue. She strutted up and down, carefully imitating masculine gestures and trying to take long strides.

Suddenly, she changed her mind.

'I am not going,' she decided. 'What if someone should see through my disguise? And your parents—they would never allow me to go alone with you.' I urged her to change her mind and go with me.

'Everyone at the temple knows me,' I persisted. 'Even if anyone should recognize you, he would only laugh at you. As Mother is away visiting Ninth Sister and her husband, we could leave and come back in secret, with no one any the wiser.'

Looking at her reflection in the mirror, Yuen shook with repressed laughter, until I took her by the arm and pulled her after me. In silence, then, we stole from the house without meeting a soul.

Arrived at the temple, we roamed around the grounds, causing no comment; no one recognizing Yuen nor guessing that she was not a man. When I introduced her to my friends as a visiting boy cousin, they only bowed politely and passed on. Late in the evening we reached a place where several ladies and young girls were sitting beside their floral display. Remembering them as members of the family of the exhibitor, Mr. Wang, Yuen hurried over to talk to them. They were very cordial to her until, in the course of the conversation, she leant over and thoughtlessly put her hand on the shoulder of one of the young ladies. This was a serious breach of good manners and angered the elderly servant who was sitting beside the girl.

'You young rascal,' she shouted at the supposed young man; 'how dare you take such a liberty!' Before I could step forward to explain and smooth things over, Yuen, realizing the seriousness of the situation, had pulled off her hat and raised her foot in its butterfly shoe.

'Look!' she cried. 'I too am a woman!'

After the first few moments of surprise, their anger gave way to amusement and the whole family insisted on entertaining us with tea and cakes until I called a sedan chair to return home.

For the Festival of Hungry Ghosts, on the fifteenth night of the seventh month, Yuen prepared a little feast in honour of those poor, unhappy spirits who have no living descendants to burn incense before their spirit-tablets. We were eating on the balcony of the pavilion and had invited the moon to drink with us, making a third at our celebration. Our cups were raised to drink the first toast, when suddenly, from nowhere it seemed, ominous clouds massed above our heads, darkening the clear sky and obscuring the face of our guest, the moon. Yuen shivered and turned pale.

'If the Gods mean that you and I are to grow white-headed together,' she whispered, 'the moon must come out again tonight!'

I, too, felt depressed and apprehensive, looking across the water to the darkness of the opposite shore, where will-o'-the-wisps, shining in the blackness like thousands of tiny, bright lanterns, wove in and out among the tangled willows. To dispel our fears and depression we began composing poetry, one of us starting a verse, the other finishing it; each composing a couplet in turn. Rhyming back and forth, we began to let our imagination run wild; indulging our most foolish fancies until we found ourselves laughing hysterically at the most ridiculous nonsense verses. Yuen choked and gasped, tears streaming down her cheeks. Breathless at last, she leant her head against my chest, filling the air with the fragrance of jasmine from her hair.

'I know that from ancient times jasmine has been the favourite ornament for women's hair,' I said, patting her on the back to stop her choking; 'but I had always thought that it was used because the flowers had the colour and beauty of pearls. I had no idea that its fragrance was so enhanced when it blended with the perfumes of hair oil and face powder. When jasmine smells like this, even the citron must take second place.'

The choking had stopped now, and Yuen was resting, exhausted, in my arms.

'The citron is the aristocrat of perfumes,' she said; 'its fragrance is so subtle and elusive. But jasmine is a peasant, borrowing part of its personality from others; like a sycophant, it laughs and shrugs its shoulders while it insincerely curries favour.'

'Why then,' I asked her, 'does my darling avoid the aristocrat and associate with the peasant?'

'The aristocrat pleases me, I suppose,' she replied; 'but I love the peasant.'

As we talked, the third watch was drawing to a close, the wind was gradually sweeping away the clouds, and when the moon burst forth again in silver radiance, happiness once more filled our hearts. Standing by the window, we raised our cups in toasts to the moon and to each other. We were drinking the second toast when a commotion broke out under the bridge. Then we heard what sounded like a loud splash, as if someone had fallen into the water, but when we rushed to the window and looked down into the stream, there was nothing unusual to be seen. The water was as clear and smooth as a mirror. Not a sound now broke the stillness but the cry of a scurrying duck on the opposite bank. (I had always known that the gardens of the Ts'ang-lang Pavilion were haunted by the ghost of a man who had drowned in the canal, but, because of Yuen's fear of the supernatural, I had not dared to tell her about it.)

'Oh! That frightening noise!' Yuen cried, shuddering with terror. 'What was it? Where did it come from?'

Horror-struck—our bodies trembling uncontrollably—we hastily closed the window and carried the wine into the room, where the gauze curtains hung motionless and the lamp-flame had shrunk to the size of a pea. Like the frightened man in the old story, 'seeing the bow's reflection as a snake's shadow in wine-cup', I nervously raised the lamp-wick and crept behind the curtains of the bed. There I found that Yuen was shivering and burning by turns. Before long, I too had developed a high fever.

For the next twenty days or so we lay in bed, exhausted and feverish, a prey to nameless fears.

How true is the ancient saying: 'When happiness reaches its peak, calamity is sure to follow.' The events of that terrible night seemed to be still another omen that we two should never grow old together.

Not until the arrival of the Harvest Festival, on the fifteenth day of the eighth month, were we feeling well enough to leave our room again. At that time, although six months had passed since Yuen's coming to my home as a bride, she had never gone next door to see the Ts'ang-lang Pavilion itself; so I now sent a servant to ask that the watchman close the gates to visitors for the rest of the day. At twilight, following an old servant who went ahead to lead the way, I went to the gardens with Yuen, a maid to help her, and my youngest sister and her nurse.

Crossing a stone bridge, we went through a gate, turned east, and followed a winding path into the garden, walking between artificial hills of piled-up rocks and through groves of lush green trees, until at last we climbed the steps to the Pavilion, set high on a hill at the heart of the place. From this elevation, as far as the eye could see, the land fell away to the horizon in every direction. Smoke was rising from the cooking fires of the houses far below, curling upwards against a background of brilliantly-coloured sunset clouds. We could see, on the opposite bank, a grove of trees called 'the Forest by the Mountain'; a spot where high officials often entertained gatherings of friends.

We had brought along a rug to spread on the floor of the Pavilion and were sitting on it now while the watchman served us tea. The moon had already silvered the tops of the trees. The first stirrings of a breeze played up the sleeves of my gown, and as I watched the moon's reflection in the rippling water, my heart was freed of all its troubles and anxieties. How unimportant, at that moment, seemed the pursuit of fame, the pangs of love; how trivial the small successes and failures of everyday life!

'This has been such a wonderful evening,' Yuen sighed. 'If only we could take a little boat and go drifting through the garden for ever and ever, without changing or growing any older! Wouldn't that be perfect happiness!'

Night was falling. Lamps were shining from the houses below. I remembered our frightening experience on the Festival of Hungry Ghosts and suggested that we leave the Pavilion and start on our way home.

It was the custom in Soochow, on the night of the Harvest Festival, for women of all classes, from great families and 'small doors' alike, to take a stroll together in the moonlight; a ceremony called 'footsteps of moonlit harmony'. But, despite the beauties of the neighbourhood of the Ts'ang-lang Pavilion, we met no walking parties going in the direction of the gardens.

CHAPTER 4

As my father took delight in adopting sons, I had twenty-six older and younger brothers with surnames different from mine. My mother had adopted nine daughters, two of whom, Second-cousin Wang and Sixth-cousin Yu, became very fond of Yuen. Wang was a hoyden. More like a boy than a girl, she was wild and impetuous, with a great liking and capacity for wine. Yu was a cheerful girl, carefree and honest, and a great chatterbox.

Whenever Wang and Yu were visiting Yuen they insisted on my spending the night with one of my brothers, so that all three girls could share the same bed. This plan, I was sure, had been devised by Miss Yu.

'After you get married,' I threatened her, 'I shall invite your husband here and keep him with me for ten whole days. How will you enjoy that?'

'I shall come here too,' Yu said. 'I'll stay and go to bed with Yuen. Wouldn't that be exciting!' At this, a slight smile passed between Yuen and Wang, but neither of them made any comment on Yu's nonsense.

After the marriage of my brother Ch'i-t'ang, our family moved to a house near the Bridge of Drinking Horses, in Rice Granary Lane. Our new home was large and pleasant, but it lacked the elegance and seclusion of the old one near the Ts'ang-lang Pavilion. In honour of my mother's birthday, we had a theatrical performance in the garden of the new house. Yuen at first thought it a rare and exciting experience, until my father, who was not a superstitious man, called for a tragic piece called *The Sorrows of Parting*. In this play, the actors played their parts so well, presenting such a true picture, that their audience was very much affected. Before the scene was over, I saw Yuen rise and unobtrusively leave the garden. When she did not come back again, I went into the house to look for her, with Yu and Wang behind me.

We found Yuen alone in her room, leaning on her dressing-table, supporting her cheek with her hand.

'What has made you so unhappy?' I asked her.

'I thought that plays were supposed to be amusing and entertaining,' she answered; 'but today's play has broken my heart.'

Yu and Wang broke into amused laughter.

'Yuen is upset because she is sensitive and emotional,' I said angrily. 'She feels everything very deeply.'

'Then ask your sensitive wife if she intends to sit in here alone for the rest of the performance,' Yu laughed.

'If there is a play worth seeing,' Yuen said, 'then I'll go out and watch it.'

25

When she heard this, Wang went to my mother and asked her to choose only amusing plays like *Chih Liang*, and *Hou So*; after this, Yuen was persuaded to come out again, and, before long, she had recovered her former high spirits.

My father's brother Su-ch'un dying when he was young, and leaving no heir, my father had made me his adopted son, in this way assuring my uncle of descendants to perform the rights before his ancestral tablet. Su-ch'un was buried in the family graveyard on the Hill of Happiness and Longevity at Hsi K'ua Tang, and every year, at the Ch'ing Ming Festival, Yuen and I went there for the ceremony of sweeping the graves. When she heard there was a superlative garden near the tombs, a famous beauty spot called the 'Garden of Spears', Wang asked to be allowed to go with us.

Scattered on the hillside, at the tombs, Yuen noticed some stones that were moss-grown and streaked with colour. Excited by their beauty, she pointed them out to me, suggesting that we collect them to make a grotto in our garden at home.

'These are much more beautiful and far older-looking than the white stones from Hsüan district,' she said.

I told her I thought it would be difficult to find enough of these particular stones.

'If Yuen would really like them, I'll collect them for her,' Wang offered.

Borrowing a sack from one of the watchmen, she began to pick them up, hopping about with 'stork's steps', holding out each stone for my inspection as she found it. If I approved its shape and colour, she would drop it in the bag; if I said 'no good', she would throw it away again. In a short time she came over, dragging the sack, her face-powder streaked with perspiration.

'I haven't the strength to pick up one more stone,' she panted.

26

Idly, Yuen began sorting out the best stones.

'They say you have to be a monkey to gather mountain fruits (stones),' she laughed; 'and I see that it is quite true!'

Enraged, Wang rushed at Yuen with fingers curved as if to scratch the smile from her face. Coming between them, I scolded Yuen angrily.

'You sit there doing nothing while Wang does all the work,' I said. 'Can you blame her for resenting your spiteful remarks?'

On the way home we visited the 'Garden of Spears', a place all delicate greens and clear reds, where each flower and tree seemed to be trying to outshine the rest in brilliance and beauty. The childish and undisciplined Wang could not resist the urge to pick every flower she saw. Yuen became very annoyed with her.

'Why must you pick so many flowers?' she asked.

'You know you have no intention of taking them home for the vases or of wearing them in your hair.'

'Flowers aren't sensitive to pain,' Wang said. 'I'm not hurting them, so what does it matter?'

'The flowers will have their revenge in the future,' I said laughingly, 'when you are given in marriage to a pock-marked man with long whiskers!' Wang gave me a furious look, threw the flowers to the ground and kicked them into the middle of a pond.

'Why are you both so rude to me?' she wailed. Yuen began to laugh then and finally succeeded in calming Wang and restoring peace.

My brother Ch'i-tang's wife, dressing too hastily one morning, accidently broke her pearl hairpin, and Yuen brought out her own pearl hair ornaments, which had been her betrothal presents, asking my mother to give them to the young bride.

'What a shame!' said one of the servants. 'You should not give your pearls away.'

'Women are the incarnation of the "yin" principle,' Yuen said to her, 'the feminine principle, dark and secret; and pearls, also, are the essence of the female. For a woman to wear pearls is for her to subdue completely the "yang", the male principle, the positive side of her nature, the aspect of life and light. For this reason, pearls have no value for me.'

But old, torn books and fragments of paintings, these things Yuen prized and loved. After carefully sorting the tattered, dirty books, she would set to work cleaning and repairing the torn pages, afterwards collating the volumes, rearranging them in sets and having cases made for the complete ones. She called this collection 'Treasured Leaves and Fragments'.

Damaged paintings, too, and calligraphic scrolls she carefully restored, searching until she found old matching silk and paper for repairing the tears and holes. Then she would ask me to fill in any missing places with my brush, before she lovingly rolled them and stored them away. These scrolls she labelled 'Discarded Treasures Collected and Enjoyed'. From the continual petty irritations of her days, from her sewing and the labour of supervising the kitchen, Yuen found rest and peace in restoring her books and scrolls. Happening to find an old book in a forgotten chest or a worthwhile piece of calligraphy among some discarded papers, she was as happy as if she had come upon a rare treasure.

My wife and I had quickly discovered ourselves to have identical tastes and habits. Invariably we liked and disliked the same things, and all our ways of thought and points of view were in agreement. She could read my thoughts in my eyes, and understand the meaning of a raised eyebrow; a glance from me was the only hint she needed to carry out the unspoken wish, to comprehend the subtlest idea.

'What a pity you were born a woman and always have to remain at home,' I complained to her. 'If only we could transform you into a man, we could roam the whole country together, visiting the Five Sacred Mountains and discovering for ourselves all the most famous beauty spots. But we can never do this, darling, because you are a woman.'

'Why can't we?' Yuen asked. 'Wait until the grey hair streaks my temples; then we can travel together and no one will object. Even if we cannot go as far as the Five Sacred Mountains and other distant places, we can surely visit Tiger Hill and the Caves of the Genie. We could go as far south as the West Lake and north as far as P'ing Shan. There are so many beautiful places that we could enjoy together.'

'By the time your hair is grey even those few steps will be beyond your strength,' I answered sadly.

'If I can't go with you in this life, then I must wait for my next incarnation.'

'In your next life, sweetheart, you must be born the man,' I said; 'then I shall be the woman and you will make me your wife. We shall live a long, happy life together and I shall delight in obeying your slightest wish.'

'We must not forget our experiences in this life,' Yuen said. 'We must be sure to remember all our former emotions too; all our feelings of love and desire. If we are conscious of both lives at the same time, think how beautiful and interesting it will be.'

I smiled and said, 'When we were children, a bowl of congee was enough to start an endless conversation. In our next incarnation, if we remember everything that happened in this one, we shall not close our eyes on our wedding night.'

'I was taught that the Old Man in the Moon is in charge of the affairs of love and marriage,' Yuen said, 'and that he joins with an invisible thread those couples who are destined to be married to one another. Since it was he who made us man and wife in this life, and in all our future lives we shall be dependent on his magic powers to keep us together, why don't we have his portrait painted and offer sacrifices to him?'

I asked a famous portrait painter, Ch'i Liu-t'i of T'iao-ch'i, to paint us a portrait of the god; showing him with ruddy face and snowy hair, rushing through the misty vapours of empty space, a red silk thread in one hand, and in the other a staff from which hung the Record Book of Marriages. When he had finished it, the figure of the god had a strength and vitality of which even a great painter like Ch'i might well be proud. After my friend Shih Ch'o-t'ang had added some verses in praise of the painting, we hung it on the wall of our room, and on the first and fifteenth of every month Yuen and I used to burn incense and pray together before it.

Because of all the misfortune that has disrupted my family, the picture has been misplaced, and now I do not know where it is.

'When this life ends, who can foretell the next?' Will the god grant the prayers of two foolish lovers? Who knows?

When we moved to the house in Rice Granary Lane I wrote an inscription on a tablet over the door of our upstairs bedroom which read 'Tower of My Guest's Fragrance'; ('fragrance' being a reference to the meaning of the name 'Yuen', 'fragrant herb', and 'guest' expressing the idea that we were always as polite to each other as guests).

The new house was not one that we would have chosen. The courtyards were too small and the walls too high. The library was in the rear, beyond another small house, and through its windows could be seen the neglected garden of the Lu family; a desolate, overgrown place which reminded Yuen, in spite of the contrast, of how much she missed the beautiful outlook at the Ts'ang-lang Pavilion.

East of the Gold Mother Bridge and north of Irrigation Channel Lane, an old woman lived in a house with a bamboo gate; a small cottage surrounded on all sides by orchards and vegetable gardens. Beyond the gate lay a pond about two hundred and fifty paces across, bordered by brilliant flowers, shady trees and tangled masses of bamboo.

The place had formerly been the garden of the famous rebel and salt-smuggler Chang Shih-ch'eng of the Yuan dynasty, who built himself a palace on the site, after proclaiming himself a prince and capturing the city of Soochow, in the year 1356.

A short distance west of the cottage a mass of broken tile and rubble formed an artificial hill, from the top of which the surrounding country could be seen, a sparsely settled region of wild uncultivated heath, broken here and there by clumps of tangled willows and bamboo.

After the old woman had once casually mentioned the place, Yuen could not put it out of her mind. Finally, she spoke about it to me.

'Ever since leaving the Ts'ang-lang Pavilion,' she said, 'I have seen it every night in my dreams. But, as we can't go back to live there, perhaps we should try to consider a second best. What would you think of this old woman's house?'

'As we are still facing the worst heat of the summer,' I answered, 'I have already thought of looking for a cool, refreshing place to spend the long, hot days. If this house really appeals to you, darling, I shall go and see if it is fit to live in. If it is, we can easily move our clothes and bedding over there and take a month's holiday. Would that please you?'

'I'm afraid your parents will never allow it,' Yuen replied.

'In this case,' I said, 'I mean to ask them myself.'

Next day, when I arrived at the house, I found that it was a small place of only two rooms, each divided down the centre by a partition running from front to back. I could see at once that with paper windows and bamboo beds it would be a delightfully cool and quiet retreat; and when I told the old woman what I had in mind, she gladly vacated her bedroom and rented it to me.

By pasting white paper on the walls, I managed to change the appearance of the room completely and to make it look fresh and clean. Then I told my mother about the place and went to live there with Yuen.

Our only neighbours were an elderly couple who raised vegetables for the markets in the city. Learning that we were staying there to avoid the summer heat, and being anxious to see that we were comfortably settled, they came to pay us a visit, bringing as a present some fish from the pond and fresh vegetables from their garden. I tried to pay them for the vegetables, but they refused to take any money. When Yuen made them a pair of shoes in return for their kindness, however, they accepted them with gratitude.

We were in the seventh month, when the trees cast dense green shadows, breezes ruffled the surface of the pond, and the din of the cicadas was deafening.

Our neighbour had made us bamboo fishing-poles and Yuen and I used to go fishing every day, in a cool, shady place under the willows. Then, at twilight, we would climb to the top of the mound to watch the sunset's afterglow reflected on the gold and crimson clouds. If we felt inspired, we might begin composing poetry; reciting couplets like this one:

> Wild-beast clouds have swallowed the setting sun,
> and now the moon's bow shoots the falling stars.

After the moon had engraved her image on the surface of the pond and the crickets had started to chirp, I would carry out a bamboo couch and set it beside the hedge for us to sit on. When the old woman told us our wine was warmed and our supper cooked, we would sit there in the moonlight, laughing and drinking toast after toast until we were often not a little drunk before beginning to eat.

After dinner we would bathe, put on cool sandals, take our palm-leaf fans and go outside again. Lying on the couch, we

風霜壓百草雷雨起雙芊 南田

3. Chinese painting by Yün Shou-p'ing (1633–1690). From an
album leaf in the William Rockhill Nelson Gallery of Art,
Kansas City, Missouri.

4. Chinese painting by Kung Hsien (Kung Pan-chien), active about 1660–1700. From a handscroll in the William Rockhill Nelson Gallery of Art, Kansas City, Missouri.

waited until our two old neighbours arrived and began to while away the night with ancient tales of rewards and punishments, and deeds of bravery and steadfast devotion to duty. At midnight, feeling delightfully cool and refreshed, we went inside to bed, almost unable to believe that we were still living in the middle of the city.

I had asked our neighbour to buy us some chrysanthemums and plant them along the bamboo hedge. When the plants began to bloom, in the ninth month, Yuen and I decided to stay for another ten days or so to enjoy their beauty and to send for my mother to come and see them also. The invitation pleased my mother and after she arrived we spent the whole day in front of the flowers, eating crab-legs and gossiping. This delighted Yuen.

'Some day we must build a house out here,' she said. 'We will have a diviner pick a lucky spot and then buy several acres of land for the house and gardens. We'll set our servant to planting vegetables and melons; then we can use the income for our living expenses. You can paint and I can do needlework to buy the wine for entertaining our friends. If we wear cheap cotton clothes and eat the vegetables from our own garden, we can spend our lives here together in perfect happiness. You would never have to travel to far places again, nor leave me at home alone.'

How profoundly I wish that her dream had come true! But now, though the place is still in existence, the one who knew my innermost heart is dead. What a tragic and pitiful loss!

After the death of Mr. Ch'ien Shih-chu of Wu-chiang, I received a letter from my father asking me to go to his friend's funeral. Yuen took me aside and asked if she could go with me.

'You will be passing the T'ai Hu on your way to Wu-chiang,' she said, 'and I have always longed to see a wide expanse of water like the Great Lake.'

'I am not looking forward to the loneliness of travelling without you,' I answered. 'It would be wonderful if you could go with me, darling, but I cannot think what excuse to give to my mother.'

'I had better say that I want to go home to see my mother,' Yuen said. 'You go on ahead to the boat and I'll follow and meet you there later.'

'If you do come,' I said, 'we should plan to anchor at the Bridge of Ten Thousand Years on the way home. We could wait to watch the moon rise, and perhaps finish the poems we began that night last year, when we were watching the moon at the Ts'ang-lang Pavilion.'

Rising early the following morning, the eighteenth day of the sixth month, I went with a servant to the Distant River Ferry and boarded the boat to wait for Yuen, who arrived, before long, in a sedan chair. Shortly afterwards, the boat cast off; and after passing Roaring Tiger Bridge we began to see sailing boats, and sand birds, and water stretching to join the sky in one wide expanse of blue.

'So this is the Great Lake!' Yuen cried. 'Now I can at last comprehend the immensity of the universe! My life has gained new meaning! But think of all the women who never leave their own courtyards; who must spend their whole lives without once enjoying a sight like this.'

While we were talking, I saw the wind-swayed willows on the banks and knew that we had reached Wu-chiang. I lost no time, but climbed ashore at once, made my appearance at the funeral and returned to the boat again the moment I could do so. To my dismay, I found the cabin dark and empty. Anxiously, I asked the boatman what had become of Yuen.

'Don't you see someone down by the bridge,' he said, pointing to the shore; 'over there—in the shade of the willows—watching the cormorant fishers?'

Yuen had already climbed the bank with the boatman's daughter, and when I joined them, I saw that Yuen's face-powder was streaked and she was bathed in perspiration. Leaning on the girl, she stood there with a far-away look on her face, and seemed quite unaware of her surroundings.

'Darling, you are soaking wet,' I said, touching her on the shoulder. Yuen turned her head.

'I was afraid someone from the Ch'ien family might come down to the boat,' she said; 'so I left to avoid any chance of a meeting. But why did you come back so soon?'

'To catch that philandering Ch'ien, of course!' I laughed, taking her hand and starting back to the boat.

When we reached the Bridge of Ten Thousand Years again, the sun was low in the sky. Dropping the cabin windows all the way to take advantage of the cool breeze, we sat there in our thin clothes, fanning ourselves and eating slices of melon to distract our minds from the heat.

At one moment the bridge was a shining crimson in the reflected glow of the setting sun; the next, a mist had begun to hide the willows on the bank. Then, before the Silver Toad in the Moon had started to show his face, the flames of the fishermen's fires began to light up the whole river.

The boatman's daughter, Su-yin, was an old drinking companion of mine. She was quite an unusual girl, and, after I had sent my servant astern to have a drink with the boatman, I called her to come and sit with Yuen and me in the bow of the boat. I had not had the lanterns lit, preferring to sit there in darkness, waiting for the moon to rise; filling and refilling our wine cups as Yuen and I played a game of forfeits.

Su-yin listened intently for some time before she said:

'I am quite good at wine games, but I confess I cannot follow this one. I have never heard it before. Would you explain it to me?'

Yuen tried to enlighten her, using all sorts of analogies and illustrative phrases, but Su-yin remained as ignorant as before.

'If Madame Professor will cease expounding,' I laughed, 'I will give Su-yin a simple illustration which will explain the matter clearly.'

'Just how do you propose to illustrate it?' Yuen asked.

'The crane is an expert dancer,' I replied, 'but cannot plough. The ox knows how to plough, but cannot dance. That is the natural order of things. To reverse that order, to try and teach the ox to dance, would be a waste of time and trouble.' Su-yin laughed.

'You mean to infer that I am stupid,' she said, hitting me on the shoulder.

'After this,' Yuen broke in sharply, 'let us settle arguments with words, not blows; by using our mouths instead of our hands. Whoever disobeys this rule must drink a large cup of wine.'

Su-yin, whose capacity for wine was heroic, poured herself a full cup and drank it in one breath.

'We should be permitted to use the hands for feeling and stroking, but not for hitting,' I said jokingly.

Yuen playfully pushed Su-yin into my arms.

'Feel her and stroke her as much as you like,' she said.

'What a silly girl you are, darling,' I answered. 'Love-making must be spontaneous, born of mutual desire. Lovers should be only semi-conscious; here and not-here. Love-making must come naturally or there is no pleasure in it. Only a boor grabs a woman and at once begins to caress her.'

The fragrance of jasmine from the hair of the two girls suffused the air, combining with the odours of face powder, wine fumes, perspiration, and hair-oil to make a perfume both subtle and exciting.

'The smell of the peasant fills the bow of the boat,' I said jokingly to Yuen. 'It is so strong it disgusts me.'

Su-yin sprang from my arms and started punching me with her closed fists.

'You profligate!' she screamed angrily. 'Who told you to smell me.'

'You have broken the rule,' Yuen called in a loud voice. 'I fine you two large cups of wine.'

'He insulted me by calling me a peasant,' Su-yin raged. 'Why shouldn't I punch him?'

'When he referred to "the peasant",' Yuen said quietly, 'he was speaking of something you know nothing about. Drink the two forfeits and then I shall tell you the story.'

After Su-yin had poured the two cups down, one right after the other, Yuen told her of our discussion about jasmine and citron, peasant and aristocrat, which had taken place the previous summer at the Ts'ang-lang Pavilion.

'In that case,' Su-yin conceded, 'I have blamed the wrong person. It was all my fault. I should be fined again.'

A third time, she emptied a large cup of wine.

'For a long time, Miss Su,' Yuen said now, 'I have been hearing of your talent as a singer. Would you sing a song or two for us?'

For answer, the girl took up a pair of ivory chopsticks, commenced beating time on the edge of a bowl, and then started to sing.

Yuen sat drinking and listening until, without realizing it, she had become very drunk. I hired a sedan chair and sent her home without me, while I stayed a little longer in the pleasant company of Su-yin. Later on, I walked home alone in the moonlight.

At the time when this took place, we were staying with my friend, Lu Pan-fang, at his home, 'The Pavilion of the Tranquil Heart'; and several days later, when Mrs. Lu heard a garbled version of the evening's events, she told Yuen about it in confidence.

'Your husband was drinking and making love with two sing-song girls a few nights ago, in a boat at the Bridge of Ten Thousand Years,' she said. 'Did you know about it?'

'I know that one of the sing-song girls bore a remarkable resemblance to me,' Yuen laughed and began to tell Mrs. Lu the story from beginning to end. Mrs. Lu enjoyed it immensely and had a hearty laugh at herself and her ill-founded suspicions.

CHAPTER 5

WHILE we were living like wandering immortals, at the Pavilion of the Tranquil Heart, my cousin's husband, Hsü Hsiu-feng, returned from Kuang-tung and saw that I was out of a job again.

'How long do you think you can exist like this?' he asked with warm-hearted concern—'trying to make a living by ploughing with your pen—breakfasting on the morning dew! Why don't you come back to Ling-nan (Canton) with me? I know there is a lot of money to be made there.'

Yuen advised me to take advantage of the opportunity.

'Go now, while your parents are in good health and you are still a young man,' she said. 'You may even find some pleasure in the business of buying and selling. Nothing could be worse for you than enduring the weariness and monotony of enforced idleness.'

Then I went to my friends for advice, and finally, with their help raised the necessary capital for the enterprise. Yuen herself managed the buying of my stock; embroidered articles, local Soochow wines, and delicacies like 'drunken crabs' (crabs steeped in wine), which were unobtainable in Kuang-tung.

On the tenth day of the tenth month, with my parents' permission, I left with Hsiu-feng for Canton, travelling by way of Tung-pa to the port of Wu-hu, in Anwhei. This being my first experience of sailing on the Yang-tze River, my heart was filled with happiness and excitement. Every evening, after we had cast anchor, I would go up to the bow of the boat and have a drink. One night I watched a man fishing with a square net no more than three feet wide, which yet had meshes at least four inches across. The net was weighted with iron hoops at each corner, which seemed to be used as sinkers. Smiling, I said to Hsiu-feng:

'The Sage tells us "Do not fish with close-meshed nets". But I cannot see how that fisherman expects to catch any fish with such large meshes and such a small net.'

'That is an especially-made net, devised to catch pien fish,' my cousin explained. The net was attached to a long rope which the fisherman now started raising and lowering at intervals, as if he were trying to catch a fish; and before long, when he pulled it quickly from the water, there was a pien fish—caught by the neck in one of the meshes, like a prisoner in a cangue.

'Seeing is believing!' I gasped in astonishment. 'But it is still a mystery to me.'

One day I saw a rocky island rising, abrupt and mountainous, from the middle of the river. Hsiu-feng told me it was the 'Little Orphan' island. I could see half-hidden temples and pavilions among the frost-covered trees, but unfortunately we could not stop to stroll around as our boat was flying swiftly past, before the wind.

When we reached the Prince T'eng Tower I found that its location had been incorrectly described in Wang Tzu-an's unreliable article, just as he moves the Tower of Venerated Classics in Soochow to the Great Wharf of the Hsu Gate! At the Prince T'eng Tower we boarded a junk with a high stern and a rising prow, known as a 'sampan', and after sailing past Kung-kuan we finally arrived at Nan-an, where we went ashore again.

The day happened to be my thirtieth birthday and Hsiu-feng made the traditional long-life noodles for my birthday dinner.

We were now travelling overland. The following day we crossed the Ta Yü Pass. The rest-house at the top of the pass had a sign board with the inscription: 'Lift your head—the sun is near', a reference to the altitude of the place. At this point, the mountain-top divided into two peaks, and the path-way ran between precipitous cliffs, which gave the impression of its being a stone alleyway.

Two stone tablets had been set up at the entrance to the pass, one reading: 'Retire with bravery before the swift current'; the other bearing the inscription: 'Be satisfied. You cannot change the past.' On the mountain top I saw a temple to a General Mei, but did not find out under what dynasty he had lived.

Why do they speak of plum flowers on this pass? I did not see a single plum tree there. Could it have been called Plum Pass after this General Mei, whose name is written with the character for plum? I was carrying some pots of plum flowers with me as presents for friends, but, as we were now in the twelfth month, the flowers had already fallen and the leaves were turning yellow.

Coming out on the far side of the pass, I saw that the land-scape was unlike anything I had ever seen before. To the west of the pass rose a hill covered with fantastic, dragon-like rocks. I forget the name of this hill, but I remember that my bearers told me there was a 'fairies' bed' on it, which I did not have the pleasure of seeing, as I was in such a hurry to reach the end of my journey. On our arrival at Nan-hsiung we hired an old dragon boat; and sailing past Fo-shan-chen, Buddha's Hill Village, I noticed that flower pots had been arranged atop the walls of many of the houses. The leaves of the plants in the pots looked like ilex, and the big red, white and pink flowers looked like peonies. These, I learned, were camelias.

On the night of the full moon, the fifteenth of the twelfth month, we reached Canton, finding lodgings inside the Ch'ing Hai Gate, where we rented three upper rooms, in a house right on the street, from a man by the name of Wang. As Hsiu-feng's customers were all local officials, I could accompany him when he went to present his credentials and make business calls; and soon after, a continuous stream of people began to arrive to select suitable presents for weddings and other ceremonial occasions until, in less than ten days, my entire stock was exhausted.

On New Year's Eve the mosquitoes were still buzzing like thunder. The people here, when they paid their New Year calls, wore thin gauze robes over their long padded gowns. Not only was the climate of Canton very different from that of Soochow, but the people themselves, although undoubtedly possessing the same five senses as the rest of the human race, yet had a different facial expression and a strange, foreign air.

On the sixteenth of the first month, when the moon was full, I happened to meet three friends from my home district who were now officials at the local yamen. They insisted on taking me down to the river to see the prostitutes; a custom known as 'making the rounds on the river'. The prostitutes were called 'lao-chü' (skilled at arousing passion).

After going out through the Ch'ing Hai Gate, my friends and I stepped into a little boat like an egg cut in half, covered over with a roof of matting, and went first to Shameen, where the floating brothels, called 'flower boats', were tied in two parallel rows, with a clear lane of water down the middle so that small boats could pass back and forth. These flower boats, in groups of ten or twenty, were moored to horizontal beams for protection against the high winds of the monsoon.

Between each pair of boats piles had been driven, to which the boats were attached by rattan rings, allowing them to rise and fall with the tide.

The procuresses here were called 'head-dress women', and wore their hair dressed high on top of their heads, coiled around hollow frames of silver wire about four inches high. Flowers decorated their temples, held in place with long ear-picks stuck into the hair behind their ears. They wore short black jackets over long trousers falling to the instep; their waists were bound with red or green sashes, and they had discarded their shoes, going bare-foot in imitation of the 'tans' of the Pear Garden, the female impersonators of the stage.

When we boarded one of the boats the head-dress woman met us with smiles and bows. Raising the curtain, she motioned us to enter the cabin, where chairs and tables were arranged along the sides, a big 'k'ang', or couch, filled the centre of the room and a door at one end gave access to the stern of the boat. After she had called out 'guests have arrived', we heard a confusion of scurrying footsteps as the prostitutes came hurrying into the cabin; some with their hair drawn up into knots, others with their braids wound round their heads, but all with their faces powdered like white-washed walls and their cheeks rouged as red as pomegranates. Some were wearing red jackets and green trousers, others had on green jackets and red trousers; some had short socks tucked into embroidered butterfly shoes, others, bare-footed, were wearing silver anklets. Squatting on the floor or leaning against the door, the girls all eyed us with interest but not one spoke a word.

Turning to Hsiu-feng, 'Why do they behave like this?' I asked him.

'After you have looked them over,' Hsiu-feng said, 'beckon to one of them and she will come over to you.'

Tentatively, I motioned to one of the girls, who immediately started towards me, smiling pleasantly and offering me a betel nut which she took from her sleeve. Putting the nut in my mouth, I commenced chewing it vigorously; but its taste was so astringent and bitter that I spat it out again at once. I tried to wipe my lips, then, with a piece of paper and saw that my saliva was red as blood, which the girls found so amusing that they all rocked with laughter.

Our next stop was at a boat called the 'Arsenal', where the girls, who were dressed and painted like those we had just left, could all, young and old, play the guitar. This seemed to be their only accomplishment, however, as the one reply they made to any attempt at conversation was 'Me-e-e?'; 'me-e-e?' in their dialect meaning 'what?'—'Wha-a-a-t?'

'They say one should never visit Canton in one's youth, for fear of being bewitched by love and beauty,' I said to Hsiu-fcng; 'but I see no danger of that in these pathetic girls, with their vulgar clothes and barbarous dialect.'

'The girls on the "Ch'ao" boats are dressed as elegantly as fairies. Why don't we wander over there?' one of my friends suggested.

At the 'Ch'ao' group, we found a double line of boats drawn up just as at Shameen; but here the procuress, the notorious Su-niang, was decked out like a circus woman and the 'powdered faces', the prostitutes, wore high-collared robes, with locks and chains around their necks. Their hair came down to their eyebrows in front, touched their shoulders in back and was drawn up on top into twin tufts like a slave girl's coiffure. Those who had bound feet wore skirts; those whose feet were natural wore short socks and butterfly shoes, which showed below the long narrow legs of their trousers. Although the dialect of these girls was understandable, I was repelled by their outlandish clothes and they, too, failed to arouse my desire.

'Across the river from the Ch'ing Hai Gate, there is a group of Yang-chow girls,' Hsiu-feng said. 'They all wear Soochow dress, and if we go over there, I am sure you can find a girl you will want to stay with.'

'Of this so-called Yang group, only the procuress, Widow Shao, and her daughter-in-law, Big Auntie, are really from Yang-chow,' one of my friends added. 'The rest of the girls are from Hu-pei, Hu-nan, Kuang-tung and Kiang-si.'

In the Yang group we found only about a dozen boats, tied in the usual double row; but everything here was familiar to me. The prostitutes were wearing their misty tresses in fluffy cloud-puffs at either side of their faces; they were delicately painted and lightly powdered; their jackets had wide sleeves; they were wearing long skirts and speaking a dialect I could understand.

After the Widow Shao had given us a cordial welcome, one of my friends, wishing to be the host, called over a wine boat, and then invited me to pick out one of the prostitutes. I chose a very young girl called Hsi-erh, whose feet were extremely small and tapering, and whose appearance and manner reminded me of Yuen. Hsiu-feng picked a girl called Tsui-ku. The others all asked for old friends.

Letting the boat drift out into the middle of the stream, we relaxed and threw off our cares; enjoying ourselves, laughing and drinking until after night had fallen.

Afraid that I might not be able to control myself much longer, I decided to go back to my lodgings, but was told that the city had been under lock and key for some hours. I had not known before that here, in the maritime provinces, city gates were always locked at sunset. Dinner over, some of my friends lay down and started smoking opium, others began hugging and teasing their girls. Soon afterwards, servants arrived with quilts and pillows and started to make up our beds; arranging them in a long row, close together, side by side. To my whispered question, 'Will you go to bed with me here on the boat?' Hsi-erh answered, 'I know of an attic we could use.

But I don't know if it is occupied or not.' (By an attic, she meant a small cabin on the upper deck of a boat.)

'Come with me then,' I told her, 'and we'll find out.'

As a sampan ferried us to the Shao boat, I saw the whole Yang group glowing with light; the two opposing rows of lanterns creating the effect of a long, shining corridor. The attic, luckily, was without a guest.

'I knew the honourable gentleman would be returning here tonight,' said the smiling procuress; 'and for that very reason, I have reserved the attic especially for you.'

'Madam,' I smiled in return, 'you are indeed the Fairy under the Lotus Leaves herself!'

A servant led us, candle in hand, to the stern of the boat, where we climbed a ladder to a small, closet-like room. The place was furnished with a bed, stools, and table which had already been prepared for us. Raising a curtain in the doorway, we entered a further room, the main cabin of the attic. Here we found another bed, off to one side, and, in the opposite wall, a square window set with glass. The room had no lamp, but was bright with the light from the lanterns of the opposite boats. All the furnishings, the bed-clothes, curtains, mirror and dressing table appeared to be very elegant and of the finest quality.

'From the rear deck,' Hsi-erh said now, 'we can see the full moon.'

Opening a window above the hatchway, we squeezed through it, snake-like, and made our way to the top of the stern, which was bounded on three sides by a low railing.

A round bright moon was mirrored in the dark expanse of water and wine boats drifted aimlessly, like floating leaves, the twinkling lights of their lanterns like stars in a second sky. Small boats wove in and out to sounds of music and singing that blended with the roar of distant waves and made my heart beat fast with excitement and emotion. How true it is, I

45

thought, that one should not visit Canton in one's youth! What a pity that my wife could not have come with me!

Turning back to Hsi-erh, I saw that she looked so much like Yuen, in the hazy moonlight, that I took her hand and led her back to the cabin. Then I blew out the candle and we went to bed together.

When dawn was beginning to lighten the sky, Hsiu-feng and the others arrived at the boat. Hastily throwing on my robe, I went out to meet them and was roundly berated for my desertion of the night before.

'I had only one reason for leaving,' I told them. 'I was afraid one of you would try to tear off the covers or pull back the curtains.'

After this, we all went back to our lodgings together.

CHAPTER 6

SEVERAL days later, Hsiu-feng and I went to visit the Sea Pearl Temple, which stands in the middle of the river and is completely enclosed within walls, like a city. On all four sides about four feet above the water, cannon protruded from embrasures, for defence against the hai-k'ou, pirates. At high tide and low tide, as the river rose and fell, the cannon seemed to rise and fall also; appearing to be always at the same distance from the level of the water. As this could not be done, it must have been an illusion.

To the west of Yu-lan Men, Secluded Orchid Gate, the buildings of the thirteen foreign firms, known as the hongs, formed a composition which looked exactly like a foreign painting. On the opposite shore stretched the Flower Garden, a place of luxuriant trees and flowering plants, the flower market of the Canton district. I have always been proud of the fact that there were few flowers I could not name; but here, in Canton, I found that I could recognize a bare six out of ten. When I asked the names of those I did not know, I found that many of them were not listed in my Botanical Dictionary, though this may have been through a confusion of names in the two different dialects.

Another temple, the Sea Screen Temple, was built on an enormous scale, and had a banyan tree inside the temple gates so large that ten men could not encircle the trunk with their arms. The tree had evergreen foliage, so dense and luxuriant that it threw a shade as dark as that from a roof. The pillars and railings, windows and thresholds of this temple were all made of iron pear-wood. A linden tree grew there also, with leaves like those of the persimmon. If the leaves of the linden are soaked in water to remove the outer skin, the fibres are then exposed, like delicate gauze cicada wings; they can then be pasted on to paper and made into little books in which to copy Buddhist sutras.

On our way home from the temple we paid a visit to Hsi-erh on the flower boat, neither she nor Tsui-ku having a guest at the moment. When we started to leave, after finishing our tea, the girls tried to keep us from going; begging us, again and again, to stay longer. It had been my idea to spend the night in the attic, until I found that it was already occupied by Big Auntie and a drinking companion. Then I asked Madame Shao if the girls could come back to our lodgings and spend the evening there with us. The procuress agreeing, Hsiu-feng went home first to make the dinner arrangements, leaving me to follow later with Tsui-ku and Hsi-erh.

Our laughter and talk being interrupted by the unexpected arrival of our friend Wang Mou-lao of the local yamen, we had just persuaded him to stay and join us in a drink when, suddenly, we heard sounds of confusion below—a great din and racket—as if a mob of people were trying to force their way upstairs.

(What had really occurred was this. The landlord's nephew, a worthless vagabond, knowing that we were entertaining prostitutes, had brought the men to our lodgings in a scheme to blackmail us.)

'This all comes of indulging San Po's sudden caprice,' Hsiu-feng said resentfully. 'I should never have followed his example.'

'Since you have already done so,' I answered, 'you had better try to help me think of a plan of action. This is no time for wrangling.'

Mou-lao offered to go down and talk to the intruders. Hurriedly summoning my servant, I sent him to hire two sedan chairs in which the girls could make their escape, and in the meantime I tried to think of a scheme by which we could get out of the city. Mou-lao not only failed to persuade the men to go away, however, but he soon returned to report that they did not intend to come upstairs. The sedan chairs arriving at this moment, I told my servant, who was an alert and agile fellow, to go down before us and open the way. Hsiu-feng followed him, leading Tsui-ku, and I brought up the rear with Hsi-erh, as, shouting loudly, we all rushed down the stairs.

With the help of one of the servants, Hsiu-feng and Tsui-ku managed to force their way through the door, but Hsi-erh had the misfortune to be caught by one of the ruffians. Quickly raising my leg, I kicked his arm until he released his hold, when Hsi-erh managed to escape. Taking advantage of the moment, I slipped through the door soon afterwards.

'Where is Hsi-erh?' I asked my servant, who was standing guard outside to prevent our being followed and overpowered.

'Tsui-ku has already left in one of the sedan chairs,' he answered; 'and I saw Miss Hsi come out, but did not see her get into the chair.'

5. Chinese painting by Hua Yen, dated in correspondence
with A.D. 1729. From an album at the Freer Gallery
of Art, Washington, D.C.

6. Chinese painting by Yün Shou-p'ing (1633–1690). From an album leaf in the William Rockhill Nelson Gallery of Art, Kansas City, Missouri.

Hastily lighting a torch, I saw the empty sedan chair still standing by the roadside. I rushed after the others then, and on reaching the Ch'ing Hai Gate, found Hsiu-feng already there, waiting beside Tsui-ku's chair. To my excited inquiries for Hsi-erh he answered: 'Perhaps she went east instead of west and is even now hurrying back again.'

I quickly retraced my steps until I had gone some ten houses beyond our lodgings, when, from a dark corner, I heard someone calling my name. By the light of my torch, I saw that it was Hsi-erh. I had helped her into the sedan chair and was about to start off when Hsiu-feng came running to tell me that there was a sluice gate at the Yu Lan Gate, through which we could get out and leave the city.

'I have already sent someone to bribe the watchman to unlock the sluice-gates,' he said. 'Tsui-ku is on her way there and Hsi-erh must start at once.'

'You go back to our lodgings and try once more to rout the invaders,' I told him. 'Leave Tsui-ku and Hsi-erh in my hands.'

We reached the sluice gates to find them already opened for us. Tsui-ku was waiting there. With my left hand I took Hsi-erh's arm, supporting Tsui-ku with my right, as we first bent over double, then hopped and staggered like cranes through the sluice.

From the skies, a light rain was falling and the roads were slippery as oil as we made our way to the river bank and came at last to Shameen, where the lights were still shining and the night was gay with music and song. Someone in a sampan recognized Tsui-ku and called to us to come aboard. Now I saw that Hsi-erh's hair was matted and tangled, and that all her hair-pins, earrings and bracelets had disappeared.

'Have you been robbed?' I asked her.

'No,' Hsi-erh smiled. 'But I was told that the things were all pure gold, and as they belonged to my foster-mother, I took

49

E

them off and hid them in my bag, before we came downstairs. If they had been stolen, you would have had to make good the loss and that would have been embarrassing for you.'

When I heard this I felt very grateful. I asked her to put her jewellery on again and to say nothing to the procuress of what had happened; suggesting she merely say that since our lodgings were so crowded we had decided to come back to the boat. Tsui-ku agreed to tell the same story.

'We have already had our dinner,' she told the Widow Shao. 'You need only bring us some rice gruel.' The former occupant having left the attic by this time, the procuress told Tsui-ku to go there with us and keep us company, and I saw, as we were climbing the ladder, that the embroidered shoes of both girls were soaking wet and caked with mud.

After eating the congee, which satisfied our hunger to some extent, we snuffed out the candles and began a long, rambling conversation in the course of which I learned that Tsui-ku came from Hu-nan and that Hsi-erh was a native of Ho-nan, her true family name being Ou-yang. After her father's death, Hsi-erh told us, her mother re-married and Hsi-erh, through the enmity of her step-uncle, was sold into prostitution.

Then Tsui-ku began to speak sadly of the bitterness of continually welcoming the new while speeding the old; of forcing laughter when the heart is sad; of being compelled to drink, though the wine made one ill; of having to entertain guests while sick and despondent; of being forced to sing with a sore, tired throat. She told of men with perverted sexual urges who would, if their demands were not acceptable, begin throwing the wine around and overturning the chairs and tables, at the same time cursing and reviling in the loudest, most abusive tones. If the procuress did not take the trouble to find out the truth, she too would berate the girl with cruel sarcasm, for her failure to satisfy the guest completely. There were other depraved men, Tsui-ku continued, men full of lust, who imposed their desires, again and again, from sunset till dawn, leaving the girl unbearably exhausted.

As Hsi-erh was very young and had just arrived, the procuress was trying to spare her as much as possible, Tsui-ku told me, crying as she spoke, the tears falling from her eyes as the words fell from her lips. Hsi-erh, too, was crying silently. I drew her onto my lap to console her, after asking Tsui-ku to go to bed in the outer room, as she was Hsiu-feng's sleeping companion.

After that evening, the girls would send a messenger, every five or ten days, asking me to visit them. Sometimes Hsi-erh would take a sampan, arriving at the river bank to welcome me in person. Whenever I went to see her, I took no one but Hsiu-feng with me. I invited no other guests nor did I visit any of the other boats.

For an evening of pleasure the cost was only four dollars. Hsiu-feng, as the saying goes, was 'today green—tomorrow red;' trying first one girl, then another; 'jumping the trough' in the slang of the flower boats. Sometimes he even went so far as to have two girls at once, but I still continued to see no one but Hsi-erh. Should it happen that I went to the boat alone, the two of us would perhaps drink a little wine on deck or talk for a while in the attic. I never asked her to sing nor insisted that she drink too much; trying to put myself in her place, I treated her with sympathy and consideration. Soon the whole boat was aware of our happiness and the other girls were all envious of Hsi-erh.

Whenever one of them had a little free time between guests, if she knew that I was in the attic, she would come up to pay me a visit, until there was not a girl on the boat who was not my friend. Each time I came aboard I was welcomed with a chorus of voices, and my eyes turned first left, then right, again and again, in response to their friendly greetings. The happiness of such moments cannot be bought for ten thousand taels. Altogether, I spent four months in Canton, throwing away about a hundred silver dollars. One of the keenest pleasures of my whole life was tasting the fresh fruit of the lichee in Canton; an experience I shall never forget. Towards the end of my stay, the procuress began insisting that I buy Hsi-erh for five hundred silver dollars, taking her as my concubine. Annoyed by her persistence, I started to make arrangements to return home.

Hsiu-feng being completely fascinated and bewitched by his life among the flower boats, I encouraged him to buy a concubine. Then we took the road by which we had come and went home to Kiang-su.

The following year, Hsiu-feng returned to Canton, but my father would not permit me to go with him. Shortly afterwards, I accepted an offer of employment from an official of Ch'ing-p'u, Mr. Yang. On my cousin's return from Canton, I learned that Hsi-erh had several times tried to kill herself because I had not gone back with him. How pitiful!

'After dreaming for six months a Yang-group dream—I awoke,
Acquiring a fickle name among the flower boats.'

The above is a paraphrase of two lines of a poem by Tu Mu:

'I awake from ten years of a Yang-chow dream—
with a fickle name among the Blue Pagodas'
(street of prostitutes).

CHAPTER 7

IN the seventh month of the year of the tiger, 1794, I returned from Kuang-tung with Hsiu-feng and the concubine he had bought in Canton. My cousin was so infatuated with his new love, praising her beauty so extravagantly, that Yuen finally accepted his invitation to go and inspect the girl for herself.

'She has beauty—but only beauty,' Yuen told Hsiu-feng later. 'She is quite without refinement or personality.'

'If your husband took a concubine, would you consider it essential that she have both beauty and personality?' Hsiu-feng asked.

'I certainly would,' Yuen replied with decision; and from that moment, it seemed, she set her loving heart on finding me the perfect concubine, despite the fact that we were far too poor to consider such a possibility.

At that time, a famous courtesan from Che-kiang province was staying in Soochow. This Wên Lêng-hsiang, 'Fragrant Solitude', had caused somewhat of a literary sensation by composing four eight-line poems on the subject of the willow catkins. Many poets and lovers of poetry had sent her their poems in reply, verses rhymed to harmonize with the originals. Chang Hsien-han, a friend of mine from Wu-chiang, who was in the habit of enjoying Lêng-hsiang's favours, brought me the 'Willow Catkins' one night, asking that I write some harmonizing stanzas in reply. Yuen, who considered the courtesan an inferior person, dismissed the idea at once, but I itched to try my skill and finally composed some verses on the same theme containing the lines:

'They arouse within me Spring's sweet sadness
And in her heart revive the parting's pain.'

Yuen thought this couplet very good.

In autumn of the following year, the year of the hare, on the fifth day of the eighth month, my mother and Yuen were preparing to visit a famous beauty spot called Tiger Hill, 'Hu Ch'iu'. Just as they were leaving, my cousin Hsien-han arrived. He too was on his way to Tiger Hill and insisted that I go with him, suggesting privately that we first pay a visit to a lady of pleasure. Without much enthusiasm, I arranged for my mother and Yuen to go on ahead, waiting for us to join them at

Pan-t'ang, near Tiger Hill. My cousin then dragged me to the house of the courtesan Lêng-hsiang.

I saw at a glance that 'Fragrant Solitude' had already reached middle age, but she had with her a young girl, Han-yuan, a virgin not yet sixteen, who looked as sweet and ripe as a melon ready for cutting. Standing there, erect as jade; chaste, dignified and beautiful; she truly reminded me of the line from Ch'uang Tzu:

'Her bright eyes, like clear pools, reflected my image in their cool depths.'

Han-yuan's task being to entertain me, I soon made the discovery that not only could she read and write but that she had some knowledge of literature as well. She also told me that she had a younger sister, Wen-yuan, who was still a child.

I had no foolish ideas at this first meeting, never allowing myself to forget that I was a poverty-stricken scholar, without the money to pay for a single cup of wine in a place like this, much less to give a dinner in return. But since I found myself there, I tried, nervous and embarrassed though I was, to enter into the spirit of the evening until I had an opportunity to take Hsien-han aside and ask him if he were amusing himself at my expense.

'Are you trying to tantalize a poor scholar with the bewitching face of a woman?' I whispered. Hsien-han smiled. 'Not at all,' he replied.

'Today I was invited by a friend to have dinner with Han-yuan, in return for a dinner of mine. But my host had forgotten an important function at which he was to be guest of honour, so I am taking his place and entertaining for him. Now will you stop worrying!' After that, I relaxed and soon began to enjoy myself.

Reaching Pan-t'ang some hours later, we met my mother's boat and drew up alongside. As Han-yuan was with us, I invited her to come with me to the other boat and be presented to my mother.

From the first instant of their meeting, Yuen and Han loved one another like old friends. They went off hand in hand to climb Tiger Hill and visit all the famous scenic spots. Yuen loved best of all the remote, high place called 'The Thousand Acres of Clouds' and the two friends sat there for a long time, enjoying the spectacular view.

Returning later to the Beach of Rustic Fragrance, we tied the two boats together, then spent a delightful evening, with much wine, talk, and laughter, before casting off again to go home.

'Would you mind going over to the other boat with Mr. Chang?' Yuen asked before we left. 'I should like to stay here with Han-yuan.'

I assented, and did not come back to my own boat until midnight, when we said goodbye to both our friends on reaching Tu-t'ing Bridge.

'At last I have found a girl who has both beauty and personality,' Yuen said on the way home.

'I have already made another engagement with Han-yuan,' she continued; 'she is coming to see me tomorrow and I shall try then to arrange everything for you.'

I stared at her in astonishment.

'But we are not wealthy people,' I said. 'We have nothing to offer her. I am just a poor scholar. Whatever put such extravagant ideas into your head? Besides, you and I are such a happy couple! Why do you want to bring in an outsider?'

Yuen smiled. 'Because I love her myself,' she said. 'But don't worry. Just leave everything to me.'

Han-yuan actually did arrive the following afternoon. Yuen treated her with touching consideration and affection, preparing a dinner for her, during which we played the guess-fingers game, the winners laughing and singing, the losers draining cup after cup of wine. All this time, not a word of the projected arrangement was mentioned, but after the girl had gone home Yuen said:

'I have secretly made another engagement with Han. She is coming here again on the eighteenth of this month, when we are going to pledge ourselves as sisters. You should provide a sacrificial feast in our honour.' Smiling, she touched the jade bracelet on her arm.

'On that day, if you see this bracelet on Han's arm,' she went on, 'you will know that everything has been arranged. I would have told her my idea before this, but I am not yet intimate enough with her.' Indulgent, I let her do as she wished.

On the eighteenth, to keep her promise to Yuen, Han-yuan braved a pouring rain. The two girls went into the bedroom, staying there for a long time. They came out at last, hand in hand. When Han saw me, she blushed with embarrassment. The bracelet, I noticed, was already on her arm.

After burning incense and swearing a solemn oath of sisterhood before the gods, Han-yuan refused my suggestion that we all drink and eat together as we had before. She said she had a professional engagement to go to Stone Lake and must leave at once.

'Now that I have found you such a beauty,' Yuen said happily, after Han had gone, 'how do you plan to reward the match-maker?'

'First tell me what you have arranged,' I said.

'I had to speak indirectly at first,' she began, 'because I was afraid that Han might have been promised to someone else. But as soon as she told me there was no one, I said to her: "Mei-mei, Little Sister, do you understand the meaning of today's ceremony?"'

'"I am truly honoured by your interest in me," Han-yuan answered, "and I would be glad to trust myself to such a beautiful and talented person; but my foster-mother has extravagant plans for me, and it would be impossible for me to make my own decision. But if you want me to come to you, perhaps, in time, we can think of a way."

'As I took the bracelet off my arm,' Yuen continued, 'I brought the subject up again.

'"I have chosen this jade bracelet, the hard stone and the uninterrupted circle, as a symbol of eternal fidelity," I told her. "Please wear it, Mei-mei, to remind you of the vows we made today."

'"Do your best to arrange it," Han said; "everything depends on you."

'Since our first meeting, Han's heart has been mine,' Yuen continued. 'It is Lêng-hsiang, her foster-mother, who will create the difficulties. But we must think of some way to manage it!'

I smiled at this and asked her playfully: 'Is my darling wife going to imitate the "Love of the Perfumed Companions", by any chance?'

Yuen smiled back. 'Yes, I am,' she said.

After this, not a day passed in which Yuen did not speak of Han-yuan. When several years had gone by, the girl was married by force to a rich and powerful man, and of all our plans, none turned out as we had hoped.

Yuen actually grieved herself to death over the loss of Han-yuan.

PART TWO

CHAPTER 8

As a young man I was excessively fond of flowers and loved to prune and shape potted plants and trees. When I met Chang Lan-p'o he began to teach me the art of training branches and supporting joints, and after I had mastered these skills, he showed me how to graft flowers. Later on, I also learned the placing of stones and designing of rockeries.

The orchid we considered the peerless flower, selecting it as much for its subtle and delicate fragrance as for its beauty and grace. Fine varieties of orchids were very difficult to find, especially those worthy of being recorded in the Botanical Register. When Lan-p'o was dying he gave me a pot of spring orchids of the lotus type, with broad white centres, perfectly even 'shoulders', and very slender stems. As the plant was a classic specimen of its type, I treasured its perfection like a piece of ancient jade. Yuen took care of it whenever my work as yamen secretary called me away from home. She always watered it herself and the plant flourished, producing a luxuriant growth of leaves and flowers.

One morning, about two years later, it suddenly withered and died. When I dug up the roots to inspect them, I saw that they were as white as jade, with many new shoots beginning to sprout. At first, I could not understand it. Was I just too unlucky, I wondered, to possess and enjoy such beauty? Sighing despondently, I dismissed the matter from my mind. But some time later I found out what had really happened. It seemed that a person who had asked for a cutting from the plant and had been refused, had then poured boiling water on it and killed it. After that, I vowed never to grow orchids again.

Azaleas were my second choice. Although the flowers had no fragrance they were very beautiful and lasted a long time. The plants were easy to trim and to train, but Yuen loved the green of the branches and leaves so much that she would not let me cut them back, and this made it difficult for me to train them to correct shapes. Unfortunately, Yuen felt this way about all the potted plants that she enjoyed.

Every year, in the autumn, I became completely devoted to the chrysanthemum. I loved to arrange the cut flowers in vases but did not like the potted plants. Not that I did not think the potted flowers beautiful, but our house having no garden, it was impossible for me to grow the plants myself, and those for sale at the market were overgrown and untrained; not at all what I would have chosen.

One day, as I was sweeping my ancestral graves in the hills, I found some very unusual stones with interesting streaks and lines running through them. I talked to Yuen about them when I went home.

'When Hsüan-chou stones are mixed with putty and arranged in white-stone dishes, the putty and stones blend well and the effect is very harmonious,' I remarked. 'These yellow stones from the hills are rugged and old-looking, but if we mix them with putty the yellow and white won't blend. All the seams and gaps will show up and the arrangement will look spotty. I wonder what else we could use instead of putty?'

'Why not pick out some of the poor, uninteresting stones and pound them to powder,' Yuen said. 'If we mix the powdered stones with the putty while it is still damp, the colour will probably match when it dries.'

After doing as she suggested, we took a rectangular I-hsing pottery dish and piled the stones and putty into a miniature mountain peak on the left side of it, with a rocky crag jutting out towards the right. On the surface of the mountain, we made criss-cross marks in the style of the rocks painted by Ni Tsan of the Yuan dynasty. This gave an effect of perspective and the finished arrangement looked very realistic—a precipitous cliff rising sharply from the rocks at the river's edge. Making a hollow in one corner of the dish, we filled it with river mud and planted it with duck-weed. Among the rocks we planted 'clouds of the pine trees', bindweed. It was several days before the whole thing was finished.

Before the end of autumn the bindweed had spread all over the mountain and hung like wistaria from the rocky cliff. The flowers, when they bloomed, were a beautiful clear red. The duckweed, too, had sprouted luxuriantly from the mud and was now a mass of snowy white. Seeing the beauty of the contrasting red and white, we could easily imagine ourselves in Fairyland.

Setting the dish under the eaves, we started discussing what should be done next, developing many themes: 'Here there should be a lake with a pavilion—' 'This spot calls for a thatched summerhouse—' 'This is the perfect place for the six-character inscription "Place of Falling Flowers and Flowing Water"'—'Here we could build our house—here go fishing—here enjoy the view'; becoming, by this time, so much a part of the tiny landscape, with its hills and ravines, that it seemed to us as if we were really going to move there to live.

One night, a couple of mis-begotten cats, fighting over food, fell off the eaves and hit the dish, knocking it off its stand and smashing it to fragments in an instant. Neither of us could help crying.

'Isn't it possible,' I sighed, 'to have even a little thing like this without incurring the envy of the gods?'

Burning incense in a quiet room is one of the subtlest delights of the life of leisure. Yuen used to make our incense from aloe and from su-hsiang, a fragrant wood from Cambodia. After first steaming it thoroughly over a pot she would place the wood on a copper-wire rack over a brazier, just about half an inch above the fire. The wood, drying slowly, then produced a subtle, delicate fragrance, without giving off any smoke.

'Buddha's Fingers' (a fragrant variety of citron often used to perfume rooms) should never be smelled by a drunken man, for fear that its odour will change, becoming putrid. The quince should be kept from perspiring, if possible. If it has perspired, it should be rinsed off in clear water. The lemon is the only fruit that may be freely handled without fear of spoiling the perfume. There are other rules for the care of 'Buddha's Fingers' and quinces which are not easily put into words. Again and again, I have seen a person pick up one of these properly kept fruits, carelessly handle and smell it, then roughly throw it aside. Such people show that they are ignorant of the proper way to treat these delicate fruits.

Simple though my life has been, I have always had a vase of flowers on my table. Yuen thought I had a real talent for flower arrangement.

'The way you create different effects; wind, clear skies, rain or dew; shows your understanding of the essence of the art,' she said. 'There is a style of painting, with grasses and insects, that you might like to imitate in your vase.'

'The insects would struggle and stagger about; I could never make them keep still,' I answered. 'I wonder what we could do to achieve the effect?'

'I know of a way to do it,' Yuen said, 'but I am afraid it would cause too much suffering to the insects.'

'Tell me about it,' I asked her.

'Since insects don't change their colours after death,' she said, 'you should find a praying mantis, a cicada and a butterfly or two; take a needle and kill them, then with fine wire attach them by their necks to the flowers and grasses. You could arrange some with their feet grasping the stems, others resting on the leaves as they do in life. Don't you think it's a good idea?'

I was delighted with it. I followed her suggestions exactly and my friends all thought the results were marvellous. Where, among all the women in the world, could I find another such sensitive and understanding heart?

While we were staying with the Hua family at Hsi-shan, Yuen taught Mrs. Hua's two daughters to read. In the court-yard of the Hua farmhouse, a wild and unfenced place, there was no protection from the discomfort of the summer sun, until Yuen showed the family how to make beautiful movable screens of growing plants. Each screen consisted of a single panel, for which Yuen used two pieces of wood about five inches long, placed side by side like a low bench, with four-foot long horizontal wooden bars fastened at right angles across the top. Into holes bored at each of the four corners she then stuck a woven bamboo trellis, making a screen six or seven feet high. Climbing beans, growing from a pot of sand in the centre, could creep and twine over the entire screen, which would even then be light enough for two people to move from one place to another.

Several of these screens were made from time to time and set up to throw a shade or screen a window. Looking like growing plants, they threw a green shade across the windows and allowed the breeze to pass through while shutting out the sun. They could be set at any angle and their positions changed according to the season or the time of day. For this reason we called them 'movable flower screens'. Any fragrant herbs or climbing weeds a locality might provide would be suitable for such a screen, which makes it very useful for a country house.

Poor scholars, with small houses and large families, would do well to follow the example of the boatmen of my native district who have worked out a clever way of extending the limited deck space at the stern of their boats. They build there a series of platforms, one above the other like steps; and these they use as beds, as many as three in a line, divided by partitions of wood and pasted paper. This is in every way a most satisfactory arrangement. As if one were walking down a long stretch of road, there is no feeling of confined space at all.

Yuen and I used this idea when we moved to Yang-chow, where our house had only four rooms, but looked both spacious and in good taste, after the bedrooms, kitchen and drawing-room had all been arranged in this way.

'Your arrangement is certainly in exquisite taste,' Yuen once said jokingly, 'but it does not give the appearance of a rich man's home.'

In this she was undoubtedly right!

My friend Lu Pan-fang, with the intimate name of Chang and the literary name of Ch'un-shan, Spring Mountain, was an accomplished painter of pine and cypress trees, plum flowers and chrysanthemums. A fine calligrapher as well, specializing in writing the li shu, or square style of characters, he was equally good at carving seals.

For a year and a half I was a guest in his home, the Pavilion of the Tranquil Heart, a two-storied house of five beams, facing towards the east. My own apartment there had three rooms. It commanded a beautiful view of the distant country-side, by night and day, in clear or stormy weather, and was pervaded by the tantalizing fragrance of the single cassia tree that grew in the middle of the courtyard. Verandas and corridors connected the rooms on the east and west sides of the court and the whole place had an atmosphere of peace and seclusion.

7. Chinese painting by Kung Hsien (Kung Pan-chien), active about 1660–1700. From a handscroll in the William Rockhill Nelson Gallery of Art, Kansas City, Missouri.

8. Chinese painting by Hua Yen, dated in correspondence
with A.D. 1729. From an album at the Freer Gallery
of Art, Washington, D.C.

When we moved to the house we took with us only two servants, an elderly man and his wife, who brought their young daughter along to help them. The man knew how to sew and the woman could spin. In consequence, while Yuen embroidered, the old woman spun and the man made clothes to help provide the money for our living expenses.

By nature I am very hospitable and have always loved to entertain. Whenever we had little dinners, I would always insist on playing wine games. Yuen was an excellent cook and turned out wonderful, inexpensive meals; the simplest dishes, of vegetables, melons, fish or shrimps, after passing through her hands, acquired the subtlest and most unexpected flavours. As my poverty was no secret, each of my friends would contribute his share of the wine money, so that we were able to spend whole days in leisurely conversation.

I liked the place kept spotlessly clean, without a trace of dust or dirt, but at the same time I liked to feel completely free and unconstrained in all my actions, wishing my friends also to do exactly as they pleased, even to the extent of indulging their wildest whims.

Among my friends at this time were Yang Pu-fan, with the intimate name of Ch'ang-shu, a painter who specialized in portraiture; Yüan Shao-yü, or Pei, a talented landscape artist; and Wang Hsing-lan, Yen, who painted plants and flowers, birds and animals. Enjoying the privacy and quiet of the Pavilion of the Tranquil Heart, they would bring their painting materials with them when they came to visit us; and from them I learned to paint.

Sometimes we wrote scrolls in grass or seal scripts, at other times we spent the hours engraving seals. The money from these pursuits we handed over to Yuen to help pay for the food and wine. We talked of nothing, all day long, but poetry and painting.

I had other friends also, like the two brothers Hsia, Tan-an and I-shan; the Miao brothers, Shan-yin and Chih-po; and

F

Chiang Yun-hsiang, Lou Chü-hsiang, Kuo Hsiao-yü, Hua Hsing-fan and Chang Hsien-han; all of them coming and going as freely as swallows on the ridge-pole.

In those days, Yuen thought nothing of quietly pulling out her hairpin and selling it to buy wine, rather than let a beautiful day pass without entertaining. Now that these friends, like clouds dispersed by the wind, have drifted to the four corners of the earth and she who was my very self is dead, like broken jade or buried incense, I find it unbearably painful to look back upon that time.

Four pastimes were taboo at the Pavilion of the Tranquil Heart: talking about official promotions and demotions— mentioning law suits or news of the day—discussing the eight-legged essays of the Imperial examinations—and disclosing one's hand by one's looks while playing cards; and anyone breaking a taboo was fined five catties of wine.

Four qualities we all cherished: a generous nature, loyal, brave and gay—an attitude cultivated and refined, yet still romantic and unconventional—a free-and-easy manner, unhampered by petty restrictions—and a tranquil spirit, possessing the gift of silence.

During the long days of summer, having nothing better to do, we used to hold examinations among ourselves. There would be eight of us in the group, each of whom had brought with him two hundred 'water beetles' or cash, and we began by drawing lots to see who would first act as Grand Examiner, seating himself apart with his official seal of office. In the same way we chose the Recorder, who would also take a seat. The rest of the party became the chü-tzu, candidates for the literary examinations, and each received from the Recorder a slip of paper properly stamped with official seals.

The Grand Examiner would then give out a five character phrase and a seven character phrase, from each of which the chü-tzu must compose a couplet, the time allotted for composition being the interval of the burning of a stick of incense.

The candidates might walk or stand while composing, but no private conversations nor whispered exchanges were permitted. The couplets completed, the candidates dropped them into a box and could then return to their seats.

After each person had handed in his finished work the Recorder would open the box and copy all the couplets into a book, which he would then present to the Grand Examiner, in this way preventing any chance of favouritism. From among the sixteen couplets, three of the five character and three of the seven character couplets would first be chosen. From these six couplets, the best of all being next selected, the winning candidate became the Grand Examiner, and the winner of second place the Recorder.

A candidate having two couplets rejected was fined twenty cash; for one rejection the fine was ten cash and for failures handed in beyond the time limit the fine was doubled. After each examination the Grand Examiner received a present of a hundred cash, or 'incense money', and as it was possible to hold as many as ten examinations in one day, we often collected more than a thousand cash, which would buy enough wine for a grand celebration. It was decided that Yuen's papers should be in a class by themselves and that she was allowed to compose while sitting down.

One day Yang Pu-fan made a sketch of Yuen and me as we were working in the garden, and caught our likenesses with remarkable skill. That night the moonlight was unusually beautiful, casting the delicate and artistic shadow of an orchid on the white-washed wall. When Hsing-lan woke up after being very drunk he saw the shadow and said:

'Pu-fan paints the likenesses of real people, but I can paint the likeness of the unreal—the shadows of flowers.'

I laughed at him.

'Will the portrait of the flower be as true as the portrait of the man, though?' I asked.

For answer, Hsing-lan took up a piece of white paper and spread it against the wall. He began by outlining the shadow cast there by the orchid, then used light and dark ink to follow the tones of the image. When we looked at it next day, we saw that though it was not really a successful painting, yet the flowers and leaves had that special quality of vagueness and melancholy that moonlight imparts. Yuen loved the painting so much that we all wrote inscriptions on it for her.

There were two places in Soochow, the South Garden and the North Garden, where the yellow rape flowers bloomed; but unfortunately neither place had a wine-seller from whom one could buy a drink. Supposing we carried a basket with us when we went there, what artistic pleasure could be gained from drinking cold wine among the flowers? Someone suggested that we try to find a wine-seller nearby; someone else argued that we should first look at the flowers and then go back to a wineshop; but neither of these alternatives would be as satisfying as drinking our warm wine in the company of the flowers.

We were undecided what to do, until Yuen said with a smile:

'All you will have to do tomorrow is provide the wine money. I shall make myself responsible for providing a stove.'

At this, the whole group started laughing and calling 'Agreed'. But after the others had gone I asked Yuen if she really meant to carry a stove along herself.

'Of course not,' she answered. 'But I have seen dumpling-sellers on the streets carrying their stoves, with their pans and all the necessities for preparing a meal; and I thought we could hire one of them to go with us. I could cook the food beforehand so that when we arrive we need only reheat it. Then we'll have everything we need, including tea and wine.'

'It would be very pleasant to have both wine and tea,' I agreed, 'but we would need a pot to boil the water for the tea.'

68

'We could take along an earthenware pot and an iron prong to slip through the handle. We could remove the dumpling-man's pan and suspend our pot over the stove on the iron prong. Add some extra fuel to boil the water—and we have our tea.'

Clapping my hands in admiration, I declared it an excellent idea.

On the street I found a dumpling-seller called Pao, who gladly agreed, for a hundred cash, to go with us the following afternoon. When our friends arrived next day and I told them of the arrangement, they all thought it very clever.

We set off after lunch, carrying our mats and cushions. Arriving at the South Garden, we picked out a shady spot under some willows and sat down on the ground in a circle. First we boiled the water and made our tea. After we had drunk it, we began to warm the wine and heat up the food that Yuen had prepared.

The day was now at its best; the breeze gentle, the sun glorious above the golden fields of rape flowers. On the paths between the rice paddies people in blue gowns with red sleeves criss-crossed back and forth; butterflies and bees were circling and darting everywhere. This alone was enough to intoxicate us, without the help of wine.

When the food was hot we sat down on the ground again, commencing to eat with hearty appetites, and, as the dumpling-man was not at all a vulgar person, insisting that he too join us in a drink. Sightseers who noticed us in passing must have thought our behaviour very strange. The wine cups were strewn in wild disorder among the dishes of half-eaten food and we were all now more than a little drunk; some of us sitting, others lying stretched full-length; some of us singing, others whistling or shouting.

When the red sun was low in the sky, I began to want some rice-gruel and sent the dumpling-man to buy some rice. After eating the congee he cooked for us, we started off for home with our bellies comfortably full.

'Did you all enjoy the picnic?' Yuen asked us.

'We did,' we all replied, 'but without Madame and her clever idea, the day would not have been nearly as much fun.'

Smiling, then, we went our separate ways.

Poor scholars, who must of necessity be economical about such things as clothes and food, houses and furniture, can try, nevertheless, to see that their surroundings are clean and in good taste. In order to be economical, the proverb says 'act in accordance with circumstances', or 'cut one's coat according to one's cloth'.

I am very fond of a little wine with my meals but I do not like elaborate food, nor too many dishes at a time. Yuen made a plum flower tray, for which she used six deep white porcelain dishes, about two inches in diameter, arranging five of them about the centre dish in the manner of a five-pointed star. When the box had been painted a light grey, the whole thing looked like a plum blossom, the tray and its cover both having indented edges, and the cover having a handle like the stem of a flower. When it was placed on the table, the tray looked like a fallen plum blossom, and the lifted cover showed the vegetables served in the petals. One of these trays, with its six different dishes, contains enough for a pleasant meal for two or three close friends. If the dishes are emptied, they can always be refilled for second helpings.

We also made another tray, a round one with a low border, which we found handy for holding our cups, chop-sticks, wine pots and such things. These trays could be carried to any place one wished and were easy to remove again afterwards. This is an example of economy in the matter of food.

Yuen used to make all my collars, socks and hats. When one of my robes was torn or worn, she would take the east to patch the west, and in this way see that my clothes were always neat and in good repair. To avoid having soiled or stained places show, I always chose clothing of quiet, dark colours. Such colours may be worn to pay visits, as well as for everyday wear at home. This is an example of economy in matters of dress.

When we arrived at the Pavilion of the Tranquil Heart, I found the darkness of our rooms depressing at first, but after I had papered the walls with white paper the place was cheerful and full of light. During the summer months all the windows were taken down and stored away, leaving the whole house, without the lattice screens, wide open to the sky.

This lack of privacy disturbed us.

'There is an old bamboo blind over there,' Yuen pointed out one day. 'Why not use it instead of a lattice?'

'What can we do with it?' I asked.

'We can take several pieces of black bamboo and join them as uprights and cross-pieces to make a rectangle large enough for a person to walk through,' she explained. 'Then cut the bamboo blind in half and hang one half from a cross-piece at about the height of a table, letting it hang from there to the ground. In the centre, put four short bamboo uprights and fasten them securely with twine. Then hang the other piece of blind from the cross-piece above.

'To adjust the blind, we can roll it and fasten it with strips of old black cloth sewn to the cross-pieces. When it is finished, it will not only give us some privacy; it will be quite nice to look at and will have cost us nothing.'

This is still another way of 'acting in accordance with circumstances'; and proves the truth of the old saw, 'odd lengths of bamboo and small pieces of wood all have their uses'.

They have indeed!

In summer, when the lotus begin to bloom, the flowers fold their petals at night and open them again in the morning. Yuen used to put a pinch of tea leaves in a little gauze bag, tuck it in the heart of one of the flowers, and leave it there until the next day. When she boiled fresh spring water and made the tea, it had an incomparable fragrance and flavour.

PART THREE

CHAPTER 9

WHY is life so full of sorrow and misfortune? Frequently, a man's troubles are all his own fault, but in my case this was not so. I am warm-hearted, I always try to keep my word and I am candid and sincere; yet these very qualities seem to have been the cause of all my troubles.

My father, also, was a generous, public-spirited man; a real knight-errant, always helping people in trouble, either marrying off their daughters for them or raising their sons as his own. He spent his money like dirt; most of it on other people.

While Yuen and I were still living at home, we had certain necessary expenses which often forced us to go to the pawn-shop. At first, we tried to make the east fill the west, then to use the left to support the right; but, as the proberb says: 'Without money, you can neither manage a house nor entertain friends.'

The gossips soon began making critical remarks about us, and finally even the members of our own family started treating us with contempt. 'To be thought virtuous, a woman must be without Talent.' How true these old proverbs are!

Although I was now the eldest, I was actually the third son born to my parents. For this reason, Yuen was called Third Young Mistress by everyone in the family, until, as time went by, they began addressing her sarcastically as Third T'ai-t'ai, Third Great Lady (meaning the head of the family). What had begun as a joke gradually became a habit, and relatives and family, young and old alike, all called her Third Great Lady. Could this have been the first sign of family discord?

In the year of the serpent, 1785, when I was an assistant to my father at the yamen in Hai-ning, Yuen used to enclose short notes to me with the rest of the family letters, and my father decided, since Yuen could write, that he would turn over to her the task of writing the family letters for my mother.

Shortly afterwards, when some gossip began circulating among the relatives, my mother suspected that it was Yuen who had been indiscreet, writing of things she should not have mentioned, and from then on, she no longer asked Yuen to write for her. Seeing a letter that was not in my wife's handwriting, my father asked me if she were sick. I wrote to ask Yuen, but received no reply to my letter. This angered my father.

'Apparently your wife will not stoop to being a substitute pen and write letters for other people,' he remarked.

When I returned home and found out the truth of the whole involved misunderstanding, I started to bring the matter out into the open to try and make peace, but Yuen anxiously stopped me.

'I would rather be in disfavour with your father than incur your mother's displeasure,' she said unhappily.

After that, I decided not to do anything further, and left things as they were.

In the spring of the year of the dog, 1790, I again went to Han-chiang (an old name for Yang-chow) to work for my father, who was secretary to an official at the yamen. A business associate of my father's, a Mr. Yu Fou-t'ing, was living at this time in Yang-chow and had brought his family there with him.

'Unfortunately, my whole life has been spent away from home, among strangers,' my father said to Yu one day. 'I have always wanted a companion to share my daily life with me, but I have not been able to find one. If my son had any real sympathy for my position, he would try to get me a concubine from my home district, whose dialect I could understand.'

When Fou-t'ing passed this information on to me, I wrote privately to Yuen, asking her to engage a match-maker to look for a concubine for my father. She did as I asked her, settling on a girl from the Yao family; but as she did not know if my father would approve her choice, Yuen decided to say nothing to my mother about it. When the girl came to Yang-chow, Yuen made the excuse that she was a girl from the neighbour-hood who was going on a pleasure trip.

After my father had asked me to bring the girl to live with him at the yamen, Yuen listened to someone's advice and told the story that my father had wanted this girl for a long time. Hearing these conflicting stories, my mother said:

'First she was a neighbourhood girl who was going on a pleasure trip! Now my husband takes her as his concubine!'

And Yuen was out of favour with my mother also.

My father fell ill in the spring of the year of the rat, 1792, and when my younger brother Ch'i-t'ang and I went to Yang-chow to take care of him, I contracted the illness also. Yuen wrote, in one of her letters to me, that Ch'i-t'ang had some time ago borrowed money from a neighbour, for which she was the guarantor, adding that the woman was now making a fuss and demanding repayment of the loan. I tried to talk to Ch'i-t'ang about it but he angrily accused my wife of meddling in his affairs; consequently, I merely added a note at the bottom of my next letter to Yuen saying that as father and I were both ill at the moment, we had no money to repay the loan. 'Wait until brother Ch'i-t'ang comes home,' I finished, 'and let him take care of his own problems.'

Before very long, I was well enough to go back to Chen-chow. Yuen's reply to my letter arriving after I had left Yang-chow, my father opened and read it. In it, Yuen had written of the affair of Ch'i-t'ang's debt to the neighbour woman and had then continued, 'Your mother regards the old man's illness as being the direct result of his taking the Yao girl as his concubine. As soon as your father begins to show signs of recovery you should secretly tell Yao to pretend that she is homesick. At this end, I shall ask her parents to go to Yang-chow and bring her home with them. After that, you and I will have no further responsibility in the matter.'

Reading all this, my father became enraged. He asked Ch'i-t'ang about the debt but my brother denied knowing anything about it. Then my father wrote to me. 'Not only has your wife borrowed money behind her husband's back,' he complained, 'but she is now spreading slander about your younger brother. She also had the impertinence to refer to her mother-in-law as "your mother" and to call me "the old man". This I regard as the most flagrant disrespect and perversity. I have already sent a special messenger to Soochow, ordering them to turn her out of the house. If you have any decent feelings yourself, you will realize that you are also to blame.'

This letter came like a clap of thunder from a clear blue sky. Answering it immediately, I accepted the entire blame for everything that had happened. Then I hired a horse and rode home as fast as I could, terrified that Yuen might try to kill herself. As soon as I arrived, I began to explain the matter from beginning to end but was soon interrupted by the entrance of the messenger with my father's letter.

In it, my father wrote angrily of Yuen's many faults and weaknesses, denouncing her behaviour in the strongest possible language. All this time Yuen sat crying silently.

'I know it was wrong of me to lie and to write disrespect-fully,' she admitted at last; 'but Father should realize that I did it through ignorance, and forgive me.'

A few days later we received another letter from my father in which he wrote: 'I have decided not to be too severe with you, but you must send your wife to live somewhere else at once. Keep her out of my sight unless you want to make me really angry.'

But if I were to send Yuen away, where could she go? Her mother was dead, her younger brother had disappeared, and she could not bear the thought of becoming a dependent in the home of some distant relative. Fortunately, my friend Lu Pan-fang heard of our situation. Feeling very sympathetic, he invited us to stay in his home, the Pavilion of the Tranquil Heart.

More than two years passed before my father found out what had really happened. Soon after I returned from Canton he came to have a talk with me at the Pavilion of the Tranquil Heart.

'Now that I understand everything,' he said then, 'why don't you come home again?'

Yuen and I were overjoyed, and returned at once, to make the family circle once more complete.

We had no idea, at the time, that the affair of Han-yuan, with all its tragic consequences, lay ahead.

CHAPTER 10

YUEN used to have female troubles, with much loss of blood, beginning when her brother K'e-ch'ang ran away from home, and becoming chronic after her mother died from incessantly brooding over her son's disappearance. Yuen's bitter sorrow had seriously affected her health, but since her friendship with

Han-yuan, more than a year had now passed without a sign of her sickness, and I was happy that she had found so effective a medicine.

Han-yuan, however, was soon to be snatched away by an influential man who offered a thousand gold pieces for the girl, and agreed to support her foster-mother as well.

'The beauty was now the property of a Sha-chih-Li' (like Chang-T'ai Liu, wife of the poet Han Hung, who was captured by a barbarian Tartar chieftain during the troubled times in the eighth century).

When I heard the news about Han-yuan, I did not dare to mention it, but Yuen went to see the girl one day and so found out about it for herself. She came home sobbing disconsolately.

'I don't understand how Han could be so unfeeling,' she wailed.

'It is you who are foolish and sentimental, darling,' I told her. 'What kind of feelings did you expect from such a common girl? Besides, she is used to a luxurious life, with expensive clothes and jade food. How could she be contented as a poor woman, with thorn hairpins and cotton skirts? It is better to lose her now than to let her make you unhappy later on.'

Again and again, I tried to console her, but until her death Yuen continued to suffer over Han's callous defection. The haemorrhages returned, becoming so severe that she had to be helped whenever she left her bed. No medicine seemed to have any effect. Then the bleeding became continuous and the bones began to show through the skin of her wasted body.

Every day, for several years, our debts kept on increasing, until people began to criticize us openly and my parents dislike of Yuen grew more and more intense, partly because of her being sworn sister to a prostitute. Standing between parents and wife, I was caught in the middle, so that whatever I did was bound to be disastrous.

Yuen had given birth to a daughter who was now fourteen years old. A clever child who knew how to read, Ch'ing-chun was also extremely kind and capable, and it made her happy to know that we relied on her to help us by pawning hairpins or clothing when we needed money. We had a son too, Feng-shen, who, at twelve years old, was studying with a tutor.

I had been out of a job for several years, since returning from Ch'ing-p'u, and finally, with my friend Ch'eng-mo, I set up a book and art shop inside my own gate. But as three days' income from the shop was insufficient to meet one day's needs, I became so anxious and weary, and lived in such poverty and distress, that I became almost too exhausted by suffering to go on living. I forced myself to endure the cold of winter without a warm gown, while Ch'ing-chun, shivering in her unlined robe, kept insisting that she did not feel cold. Because of this, Yuen vowed she would no longer have either doctor or medicine.

On one of those occasions when Yuen was able to leave her bed, it happened that my friend Chou Ch'un-hsu returned home from his duties as a secretary in the office of Prince Wang for the purpose of hiring someone to embroider a copy of the Heart Classic, the Prajnaparamita sutra. Yuen believed that embroidering a sacred text might alleviate our misfortune or even call down the blessing of Heaven upon us. The fact that the fee for embroidering the sutra was very large also appealed to her, so that she decided to do the work.

Being pressed for time, Ch'un-hsu could not wait very long for the work. In ten days, Yuen was able to tell him that the sutra was finished, but the sustained effort proved to be too much for one in her weakened condition and she began to suffer from dizzy spells and muscular pains in her back. How sad that even Buddha would not show compassion on one born to such an evil fate!

After she had finished the sutra, Yuen's illness returned with renewed force, and when she began calling first for water, then for soup or medicine, family and servants alike became wearied and bored with her.

A foreigner had rented a house just to the left of my art shop, where he made a living by fleecing those to whom he lent money at interest. Occasionally he commissioned me to do a painting and in this way I came to know him. A certain friend of mine wanted to borrow fifty gold pieces from the man and implored me to be his guarantor. For sentimental reasons I found it hard to refuse, and consented to do as he wished.

This friend later absconded with the money, going to a distant part of the country. The foreign man holding me, as guarantor, responsible for the repayment of the loan, he came to annoy me, time and time again, with his loud demands. At first, I gave him paintings in partial payment, but as time went on I had nothing left to give him. At year's end, while my father was home on a visit, the man came to the gate, shouting and creating a disturbance, demanding the return of his money.

Hearing the commotion, my father called me to him and reprimanded me severely.

'We are a family of scholars', he said to me. 'How could you fail to repay a debt to this inferior person?'

While I was explaining the truth of the matter to my father, a servant arrived to ask after Yuen's health. The man had come from a sworn sister of Yuen's childhood days, Mrs. Hua of Hsi-shan, who had heard of Yuen's illness and wanted to know how she was. Mistakenly assuming the messenger to have come from Han-yuan, my father was further infuriated.

'Your wife does not behave like a lady,' he said. 'She does not practise the feminine virtues and has become sworn sister to a prostitute. You yourself do not cultivate superior friends but associate with inferiors and undesirables. I should order you put to death, but it would break my heart to do so. I shall do nothing for the next three days. You had better hurry and make what plans you can, because if you delay longer than three days, I shall bring charges of unfilial conduct against you.'

Yuen began to cry when she heard what my father had said. 'It is all my fault that your parents are angry with you,' she said. 'My death would leave you free to go away, but I know you could not bear it if I should kill myself. And if I stayed behind,' she went on, 'I know you could not bring yourself to leave me. You had better ask Mrs. Hua's servant to come here secretly and I will force myself to get up and speak to him.'

Calling Ch'ing-chun, I asked her to help her mother dress and come outside.

'Did your mistress send you here on purpose to see me, or was it convenient to stop here on your way somewhere else?' Yuen asked the servant.

'My mistress heard some time ago that Madame was seriously ill and confined to bed,' the man replied. 'At first, she thought of coming to see you herself, but felt she should not presume to do so as she had never been to your home before. When I was leaving she told me to say that if you do not mind living in a poor and simple farmhouse, there is no reason that you should not come to the country and let her nurse you back to health, fulfilling the promise she made to you, when you were both young girls under the same lamp-light.' (The man was referring to the fact that when they were girls, doing embroidery together under the same lamp, the two women had made a vow to help each other at times of serious illness or trouble.)

'Please go home as quickly as you can,' Yuen asked the servant. 'Tell your mistress what has happened and ask her to send a boat for us, secretly, within the next two days.'

'My sworn sister Hua is fonder of me than of her own flesh and blood,' Yuen said, after the man had gone. 'It will not matter to her if you come with me, but it would be impossible to take the children too. We cannot leave them here to be a burden to your parents either. In the next two days we must make some arrangement for them also.'

At this time my cousin Wang Chin-ch'en was very anxious for his son Yün-shih to marry my daughter Ch'ing-chun.

'From what I hear,' Yuen said to me, 'the Wang's son is a spiritless weakling, without any talent or ability. He might have had wits enough to conserve the family property for his descendents, but he has no family property to conserve. However, the Wang's are a family of education and culture and he is their only son, so I suppose I must give my consent to the marriage.'

I spoke to Chin-ch'en and said:

'As you are my father's nephew I have no hesitation in betrothing Ch'ing-chun to your son, but in our present circumstances we cannot keep her with us until she grows up, before giving her to you. After my wife and I have left for Hsi-shan, you can explain our agreement to my parents, telling them you wish to take Ch'ing-chun home with you and bring her up as a virgin bride, because of the poverty of her parents. How does the idea appeal to you?'

Chin-ch'en was delighted with it.

'I shall be happy to do as you suggest,' he said.

When I approached him, my friend Hsia I-shan agreed to recommend my son Feng-shen for placement as an apprentice to learn a trade.

When all these arrangements had been completed, Mrs. Hua's boat arrived, on the twenty-fifth day of the twelfth month of the year of the monkey, 1800. Yuen was afraid that if we left openly, by the front door, the neighbours would laugh at us and make derisive remarks.

'As we never paid that foreigner his money, either,' she said, 'I don't think, if he saw us, he would allow us to leave.

We must get up before dawn tomorrow morning and steal away very quietly.'

'Can you take the risk, in your present poor health, darling?' I asked her.

'Death and life are both a matter of destiny,' Yuen answered. Don't worry about my health.'

Then I privately talked with my father, who agreed that I was doing the right thing. That evening, after first sending Feng-shen to bed, I carried our few pieces of baggage down to the boat and put them aboard.

Ch'ing-chun cried as she sat beside her mother, listening as Yuen talked to her.

'Your mother was born to an evil destiny,' Yuen was saying. I have always been too emotional and sentimental, and have loved too deeply and passionately. That is why we have all met with this disaster. But your father is kind and generous to me and after we leave you must not worry about me. In two or three years I am sure we can arrange it so that we can all be together again.

'When you go to your new home, do your very best to learn to be a good wife,' Yuen continued. 'You must not grow up to be like your mother! Your husband's parents consider themselves fortunate to have you and they will certainly be very kind to you. The things we have left in the boxes and baskets are all yours; take them with you when you go. Your brother is still so young that we have told him nothing of our plans. When we are ready to leave, we will say that we are going to see a doctor and will be back in a few days. Wait until we have been gone for a time, then explain everything to him and leave him in Grandfather's care.'

Living near us at this time was the old woman (mentioned in an earlier chapter), whose cottage we rented to escape the summer heat. As she now wanted to go with us to the country, she was in the room at the moment, sitting on one side, wiping the tears which continually streamed from her eyes.

During the fifth watch, just before dawn, we heated up some congee and the four of us ate it together.

'Long ago, we met over a bowl of congee,' Yuen said, forcing herself to smile; 'and now we are separating over another bowl of congee. If someone were writing our story as a novel he could call it *The Story of the Congee*.'

Hearing his mother's voice, Feng-shen got up.

'Where are you going, mother?' he asked, yawning.

'I am going away to visit a doctor,' Yuen answered.

'But why did you get up so early?' Feng-shen persisted.

'Because I am going a long way,' Yuen explained. 'You and your sister are both to stay at home. You must be a good boy and not displease your grandmother. Your father and I are both going away, but we will be back again in a few days.'

When the cock crowed for the third time, Yuen got up, restraining her tears, and with the old woman's help started walking to the back door. Suddenly, Feng-shen began to cry loudly.

'Oh, Mother,' he wailed, 'I know you are not coming back again!'

Afraid that his screams might arouse the neighbours, Ch'ing-chun covered his mouth with her hand and tried to comfort him, while Yuen and I stood by, feeling as if our entrails were being torn out, unable to say a word but to beg him to stop crying.

After Ch'ing-chun had finally closed the door behind us, Yuen walked some ten or twenty steps, but the effort so exhausted her that she could not go any further. Giving the lantern to the old woman to carry, I lifted Yuen onto my back and started off again. Just before we arrived at the boat we were stopped and almost arrested by a watchman of the river patrol; but, luckily, the old woman was able to convince him that Yuen was her sick daughter and I her son-in-law. Then the boatmen, who were all servants of the Hua family, hearing our voices, came to meet us and help us aboard the boat.

After we had cast off, Yuen collapsed completely, crying hysterically, unable to control her feelings any longer.

This was their last good-bye for mother and son, who were never to see one another again.

CHAPTER 11

Mr. Hua, whose given name was Ta-ch'eng, lived in a house at the foot of Tung-kao Hill, in Wu-si. A very simple, honest man, he was a farmer and ploughed his own fields. His wife, of the Hsia family, was Yuen's sworn sister.

It was past mid-day before we arrived at their house. Mrs. Hua was already 'leaning on the gate' with anticipation. Excited and impatient to welcome us, she had come down to the boat with her two little girls. They all seemed very happy to see us. Mrs. Hua carefully helped Yuen to climb the river bank and altogether gave us a most affectionate welcome.

Soon the neighbours began arriving with all their children, crowding into the house with a great deal of bustle and din. The women all stared at Yuen, asking her questions, expressing their sympathy and whispering confidences, until the whole place buzzed with the sound of their voices, like the humming of thousands of insects.

'Now I feel like the fisherman who found himself in the land of the Peachblossom Spring,' Yuen smiled to Mrs. Hua.

'Don't laugh at them, Little Sister,' Mrs. Hua replied. 'What is seldom seen is always strange and wonderful. These country women have so few opportunities of meeting anyone like you.'

Quietly and happily, we lived at the Hua house until the New Year had passed. By the fifteenth of the first month, at the time of the Yuan-hsiao festival, Yuen had so far regained her strength that she was able to leave her bed and take a few steps; and on the night of the festival, as we watched the dragon-lanterns in a large open space used for threshing wheat, I suddenly realized that she was quickly becoming her former, delightful self again.

I felt so light-hearted that I decided to have a private talk with her about our situation.

'We are living here with no plans for the future,' I said. 'I would like to leave, but as I have no money and no job, there seems to be no alternative to staying on here indefinitely. What do you think I should do?'

'I have been thinking about it too,' Yuen answered, 'and I may have a plan. Did you know that your elder sister's husband, Fan Huei-lai, is at the present time an accountant in the Salt Administration at Ching-kiang? About ten years ago, if you remember, he borrowed ten gold pieces from you. You did not have that much money at the moment and I pawned my hairpin to make up the difference. Do you recall it?'

'No,' I answered, 'I had forgotten all about it.'

'Ching-kiang is not very far from here,' Yuen continued. 'Why not go there and see him?' This seemed like a good idea and I decided to take her advice.

When I started out for Ching-kiang, on the sixteenth day of the first month of the year of the cock, 1801, the weather was so mild that even the woven cloth gown and short outer jacket I was wearing made me feel too warm. That night I found lodgings at an inn at Hsi-shan. Hiring some bedclothes, I lay down to sleep at once, knowing I had to get up at dawn to catch the passenger junk for Kiang-yin. The wind was against

us all the way and soon a drizzling rain began to fall, con-
tinuing until nightfall, when we arrived at the mouth of the
river, opposite Kiang-yin.

Chilled to the bone by the penetrating spring wind, I bought
some wine to keep out the cold, and in doing so, emptied my
purse completely. After that, I lay awake all night, undecided
what next to do, hesitating as to whether or not I should pawn
my underclothing for money to cross on the ferry to Kiang-yin.

Next day, the nineteenth, the north wind began blowing
with even greater violence and the prospects of a heavy snow-
fall seemed certain. The wretchedness of my situation had
become unbearable and in my abject misery I started to cry.
After calculating the price of the ferry ride and the expenses
for the room, I dared not buy even one drink. My cold heart
and frozen legs alike trembling, I suddenly noticed an old man
in straw sandals and woven bamboo rain hat, who carried a
yellow bag on his back and had just come into the inn.

As soon as our eyes met, we seemed to recognize one
another.

'Sir, are you not Mr. Ts'ao of T'ai-chou?' I asked him.

'Indeed I am,' he replied. 'And if it had not been for you,
I should long ago have been lying dead in some ditch! My
little daughter has now recovered her health and is always talking of your kindness to us. How surprising that we should
meet here today! What mishap keeps you here?'

(I must explain that when I was a clerk at T'ai-chou, Mr.
Ts'ao, a man of humble birth, lived there with his daughter, a
very beautiful girl, for whom a marriage had already been
arranged. As a device to get the girl for himself, an influential
man lent her father some money at an exorbitant rate of
interest, with the result that the Ts'aos were involved in a law
suit. I was able to protect the father, enabling him to return the
girl to her fiancé. Ts'ao afterwards came to my office, kow-
towing to show his gratitude and offering to serve me in any

87

way that he could. This was the man who had now come into the inn.)

I explained to him that I was on my way to visit a relative and had been detained by the heavy snow.

'If the skies clear by tomorrow, we must continue our journey together,' Ts'ao said then. Taking out some money, he bought wine for me and treated me with the utmost friendliness and courtesy. On the twentieth, when the bell for morning worship began to ring from the temple, I heard, from the river mouth, the call for passengers to board the ferry. Alarmed, I got up at once, calling Ts'ao to come with me.

'No need to hurry,' Ts'ao replied. 'We must have something to eat before boarding the boat.' After paying for my room and food he tried to persuade me to go with him to have a drink, but I had been kept there for so many days that I wanted to rush to the ferry at once. I felt I could not eat a bite, but I forced myself to swallow a couple of sesame cakes.

As we boarded the boat, a wind as sharp as an arrow was blowing from the river and my whole body was soon shaking with cold.

'I hear that a man from Kiang-yin has hanged himself at Ching-kiang,' Ts'ao came up to say, 'and his wife has engaged this boat to take her there. We have to wait for her before we can cross.'

Freezing cold, my belly empty, I waited until noon before the hawser was cast off and we started for Ching-kiang. By the time we arrived, smoke from the evening fires was rising in all four directions.

'There are two yamen at Ching-kiang. Is your relative at the one inside the city or the one outside?' Ts'ao asked.

Staggering hurriedly after him, 'I really don't know!' I said despairingly.

'Then we may as well stay here for the night,' Ts'ao answered. 'You can go and see your relative tomorrow.'

When we went into an inn, I saw that my socks and shoes were soaking wet and caked with mud. I asked to have them dried before the fire and then, without caring what I did, I swallowed a few mouthfuls of food and almost at once fell into a deep sleep of utter exhaustion. In the morning, when I got up, I found that my socks had been badly scorched by the fire. Mr. Ts'ao again paid for my food and lodging, and I left after that to look for my brother-in-law.

Inquiring first at the yamen inside the city, I learned that Huei-lai was still in bed. When he was told of my arrival he threw on his clothes and came out. Seeing the state I was in, he said with alarm: 'What is the matter, Brother-in-law? What disaster has brought you to this condition?'

'Don't ask me now,' I answered. 'But if you have any money on you, I beg you to let me have two dollars so that I can first send off the man who came here with me.'

Huei-lai handed me two foreign dollars, which I took to give to Ts'ao. At first the old man firmly refused to take anything, but I finally persuaded him to accept one dollar before he left me.

Then I described in detail to Huei-lai all the misfortunes that had plagued me on my journey and finished by telling him of my reason for coming to see him.

'You are closely related to me by marriage,' Huei-lai said, 'and even if I were not indebted to you I should still want to help you to the limit of my poor resources. But unfortunately, as our salt boats were recently robbed by pirates on the high seas and we are even now trying to assess the losses, at the moment I have very little to give you. If I manage to get together twenty foreign dollars in repayment of the old debt, would that be satisfactory?'

As I had had no great hopes of collecting much from him anyway, I said that it would be all right. Two days later the skies began to clear and the weather becoming warmer, I made plans to go home.

I arrived at the Hua house again on the twenty-fifth.

'Did you get caught in the snow storm?' Yuen asked at once, and when I told her of all the suffering I had endured she was very disheartened.

'When it began snowing, I thought you must already have reached Ching-kiang,' she said. 'But to think that you were still waiting at the mouth of the river! How fortunate though, that you happened to meet old Mr. Ts'ao. When things have reached their very worst, it seems as if Heaven takes care of good people.'

Several days after my return we got a letter from Ch'ing-chun telling us that Feng-shen had already been hired by the shop to which I-shan had recommended him and that Wang Chin-ch'en, with my father's permission, had chosen the twenty-fourth day of the first month as the auspicious time to receive her into his home. Thus, hastily and without the proper care and thought, the affairs of our son and daughter were unceremoniously settled. But to be separated from them and to remain so far apart, was to endure the sorrow and tragedy of death.

The second month began with warm days and gentle breezes. With the few dollars I had collected at Ching-kiang I went to see my old friend Hu Ch'eng-t'ang at the Yang-chow Salt Bureau and when the manager of the Revenue Department there hired me as a secretary, I began to feel a little more secure in body and spirit.

In the eighth month of the following year, the year of the dog, 1802, Yuen wrote me:

'As I have now completely recovered my health, I am very concerned about accepting food and lodging any longer from people who are neither relatives nor close friends. For a long time I have wanted to join you in Yang-chow and I should also like to see the famous scenery of P'ing-shan.'

After renting a two-room house in Yang-chow, near the river, outside the Anticipation of Spring Gate, I went to the Hua house to bring Yuen back with me. To help her with the housework and cooking, Mrs. Hua gave Yuen a young boy servant called Ah Shuang; and before we said goodbye we all promised one another that we would manage to be neighbours again some day. It was now the tenth month and as it would be bitterly cold at P'ing-shan, we decided to postpone any sight-seeing trips until the spring.

I was full of hope that we might now be able to live quietly and happily again, and that Yuen's health would continue to improve. I even began to plan for the time when our whole family would be reunited. But in less than a month the staff of the Revenue Department was unexpectedly reduced by fifteen people, and as I had only been indirectly recommended by the friend of a friend, I was consequently one of those dismissed.

Yuen at first thought up a hundred schemes to help me. She forced herself to be gay, trying to cheer and comfort me; never finding fault nor expressing resentment in the slightest degree. But in the beginning of the year of the boar, 1803, her illness returned, with severe losses of blood.

I wanted to go to Huei-lai at Ching-kiang again but Yuen discouraged me.

'It is better to ask help from a friend than from a relative,' she said.

'You are quite right,' I agreed; 'but those of our friends who care enough about us are all out of jobs too. They have no time to worry about us.'

'Fortunately the weather is quite warm now,' Yuen said. 'There is no chance that the roads will be blocked with snow. So if you must go, leave at once and come back again as fast as you can. Don't worry about me or my health. When you are disturbed and worried about me, it increases the burden of my guilt.'

As by this time I was no longer meeting the expenses of our daily life, I pretended to hire a mule in order to quiet her heart, meaning, in reality, to set off on foot with a bag of cakes on which I could nibble as I walked.

Going in a south-easterly direction I twice crossed forks in the river until, after walking about thirty miles, I came to a lonely part of the country with neither village nor house to be seen in any direction. Night was falling. Around me stretched boundless wastes of yellow sand. Above me glittered and twinkled the shining stars. I came at last upon a shrine to one of the local earth gods, a tiny shrine about five feet high, surrounded by a low wall, with two cypresses planted before it.

Facing the shrine, I kow-towed to the god and began to pray.

'I am a man called Shen, from Soochow,' I explained to the god. 'I am travelling to visit a relative and have lost my way. Finding myself in this place, I should like to borrow your shrine for the night. I implore you to have pity on me and protect me.'

Then I moved the small stone incense burner to one side and tried to crawl inside, but found the space was barely large enough for half my body. Because of the wind, I turned my cap around, pulling it down to cover my face, and sat with half my body inside the shrine and my legs, from the knees down, stretched outside it. Closing my eyes, I listened quietly to the only sound to be heard, the incessant, mournful sighing of the wind. Tired of foot and weary of spirit, it was not long before I fell into a sound sleep.

When I awoke, the eastern sky was already light and, from beyond the low wall, came the sounds of footsteps and voices. Craning my neck, I saw a group of peasants passing by on their way to a market or a fair. I asked them the way.

'Go south about three miles,' one of them directed me; 'when you reach the city of T'ai-hsing, pass through it and travel east for three miles until you reach a mound of earth.

After passing eight such mounds you will come to Ching-kiang, right on the main highway.'

Turning back to the shrine I replaced the incense burner in its original position, kow-towed to show my gratitude, and started on my way again. After passing through T'ai-hsing I was able to hire a wheelbarrow and finally arrived at Ching-kiang in the late afternoon. I sent in my card at the yamen, and after a long wait the doorkeeper came back to tell me that Mr. Fan was away at Ch'ang-chou on official business.

From his expression as he spoke it seemed to me that he was merely making an excuse and I made a point of questioning him further.

'When will Mr. Fan be back?' I asked.

'I don't know,' the man answered.

'In that case,' I returned, 'I shall wait for him, if it means waiting a year.'

The doorkeeper, understanding my inference, said quietly: 'Sir, are you really Mr. Fan's wife's brother?'

'If I were not a blood relative, do you think I would wait until he returned?' I replied.

Hearing this, the doorkeeper advised me to wait. Three days later I was told that Mr. Fan had returned and was afterwards handed twenty-five dollars with the message that my brother-in-law considered he had now fully discharged his obligation to me.

I hired a mule at once and hurried home, to find Yuen very upset; groaning and sobbing, she was crying out bitterly against the cruelty of fate. Seeing me, she burst out at once: 'Yesterday, Ah Shuang ran off with everything he could lay his hands on. I have asked everyone to look for him, but so far he has not been found.

'The loss of our things is not important, but when we left, his real mother put him in my care and begged me again and again to look after him well. If he is trying to run back home, he will have to cross the Yang-tze River and that is very dangerous. I feel so anxious about him. He may have had an accident.

'Or suppose that his parents should hide him, to try and blackmail us,' she continued. 'What should I do then? How could I face my sworn sister?'

'Darling, please stop worrying,' I begged her. 'This extreme anxiety is beyond all reason. Only wealthy people are the victims of blackmail schemes—and you and I are both destitute.'

'Furthermore,' I went on, 'since bringing the boy here a year and a half ago, we have fed him and given him clothes, and in all this time, we have never scolded him nor punished him in any way. This the neighbours all know.

'The truth is, the little wretch was simply no good. He took advantage of my absence to steal our belongings and run away. Since your sworn sister Hua gave you the little rascal, it is she who has lost face, not you. And we, on our part, should start legal proceedings at once, to forestall any trouble in the future.'

After Yuen had heard my opinion of the situation, she seemed relieved in her mind, and became much calmer; but from this time on she began having bad dreams and would cry out in her sleep: 'Ah Shuang has run away!' or 'Oh Han! How could you desert me?' Her illness grew more serious every day. I wanted to send for a doctor, but she would not let me.

'This illness was caused in the first place by my unbearable grief over the disappearance of my brother and the death of my mother soon after,' she said.

'It grew worse because of my passionate love for Han-yuan, and has been aggravated by my anger over this last disaster.

'All my life I have been over-anxious to please and too sensitive about making mistakes. I tried with my whole heart to be a good daughter-in-law but I did not succeed. As a result of my failure, I have dizzy spells and nervous heart attacks as

94

well as my other illness, which has now entered the regions below the heart and is quite hopeless. The best doctors could not cure me, so please don't waste your money on useless efforts.

'When I think of the happiness of our twenty-three years together,' she continued, 'I know that you and I have really loved each other. You have always been considerate and sympathetic to me, and have never despised me for all my stupidities and depravities. You have been not only my husband but my understanding and intimate friend; and after spending my life with you, I can die now without regrets.

'We have always been warm enough in our cotton clothes and had plenty of simple food. We have lived very happily together and been very close to one another. Sometimes, when we lived at places like the Ts'ang-lang Gardens and the Pavilion of the Tranquil Heart, we were really as happy and carefree as fairies in a heavenly world. But who were we to presume to live like fairies? Only those who have cultivated their abilities through many incarnations may expect to become Immortals. By taking what we did not deserve, you and I have angered the Creator. This is the reason we have been plagued by demons of trouble. Because you have loved me too well, who was born to an evil destiny and have brought you nothing but misfortune.'

After minutes of choking and gasping for breath she went on weakly:

'Even the man who lives a hundred years must die at last— but to part from you in the middle of our lives and be separated for ever—to be unable to be your wife to the end of your days—nor to live to see Feng-shen married—it truly breaks my heart!'

As Yuen finished speaking, tears as big as peas began rolling down her cheeks. Restraining my own feelings I tried to comfort her.

'You have been ill for eight years, darling,' I said, 'and have been at the point of death before. Why do you suddenly begin saying such pathetic, hopeless things?'

'For some time now, I have dreamed every night that my parents sent a boat to take me home,' Yuen answered, 'and every time I shut my eyes I feel as though I am floating about, as light as air—just as if I am walking through clouds and mist. I feel as if my spirit has already left and only the husk of my physical body survives.'

'Your soul has not left your body,' I told her. 'If you will take your medicine and try to rest and be cheerful, I know you will get well again.'

She started once more to choke with heart-broken sobs.

'If I had the slightest thread of vital principle left,' she gasped, 'I would not alarm you by telling you these things. But I know my dark journey to the Underworld is near and that what I do not say now will never be said.

'I know that I was the cause of all your troubles. Through me you lost your parents' love and were forced to become a homeless wanderer, beset by difficulties and poverty. But when I die, your parents will take you to their hearts again and you will forget your resentment towards them. Your parents have seen many springs and autumns; they are getting very old. After my death you should go home again as soon as you can. If you cannot take my body back to my birth-place for burial, it would do no harm to leave my coffin here for the time being, until you can take care of it later on.

'I hope you will marry again—someone both kind and beautiful, who will serve your parents and take my place with my forsaken children. Then at last I can close my eyes.'

At these words, my body felt as if it were being ripped apart, and I lost control of myself completely, crying uncontrollably, overcome with grief.

'Darling,' I cried, 'even if you were to leave me half-way through my life, I could never marry again.

'It is difficult to be water for one who has known the ocean; for one who has lost the Nymph of Wu Shan there can be no other love.'

Yuen clutched my hand tightly, trying to say something; but she could only whisper faintly 'next incarnation—next incarnation,' over and over again, until suddenly she began gasping for air, swallowing convulsively, her eyes staring fixedly ahead. I called her name 'Yuen—Yuen,' but she could no longer answer me. Like two mountain torrents the tears came pouring from her eyes until at last her panting breaths began to grow feebler and her tears to dry up, exhausted. Gradually then, she sank into unconsciousness and her spirit began that long journey from which there is no return.

From that moment, I have been utterly alone; a solitary lamp, a stranger in a strange place; my lifted eyes seeing no beloved face, my outstretched arms clasping only the empty air. This agony—this heartbreak—will it never end?

CHAPTER 12

YUEN died on the thirtieth day of the third month of the year of the boar, 1803, in the reign of the Emperor Chia-ching. My friend Hu Kên-t'eng gave me ten gold pieces to help towards the funeral expenses and with this and what I raised by selling everything in the house I managed to give her decent burial.

Alas! Yuen was a woman with a man's heart, a man's emotions, a man's talent, discernment, and understanding. From the first days of our marriage I was eternally running here and there in the struggle to make a living; but though she was often without the actual necessities of life she had the intelligence and understanding to regard their lack as unimportant. Even when it was possible for me to live at home with her, the only pleasures we had were reading and discussing literature.

That she lived on the charity of strangers and died in poverty and confusion, who can I blame but myself.

Losing her, I lost the best of all wives, the most wonderful of all lovers!

Married couples! I implore you, neither hate nor love each other too passionately, to the exclusion of all else! The ancient proverb says: 'A loving couple will never reach old age together.' Be warned by my example!

Several days after a death, tradition says, the spirit of the dead person returns again to its former home. The room, therefore, is left just as it was in the dead man's lifetime, the old clothes he wore laid out on the bed, his old shoes placed beneath it, awaiting the return of the spirit to look at them. In Kiang-su this tradition is called 'closing the eyes of the spirit'. Taoist priests are engaged for the occasion, to chant incantations, first to summon the spirit to the death-bed and then to send it away again. This ceremony of exorcism is called 'welcoming the spirit'.

In Yang-chow however, custom calls for the arrangement of sacrificial wine and food in the dead person's room, after which, everyone leaves the house, thus 'avoiding the spirit'. Because of this practice, these deserted houses are often robbed.

When it was time for the return of Yuen's spirit, my landlord, who lived in the same house, went away to 'avoid the spirit'. The next-door neighbours begged me to arrange the sacrificial dishes and leave too, but I gave them an evasive answer. I wanted to see Yuen's spirit if it returned. A man from my own district, Chang Yu-men, pleaded with me to go.

'If you allow yourself to come in contact with the spirit world,' he warned me, 'you may be entered and possessed by a demon. I really believe there are ghosts and I beg you not to make this experiment.'

'I certainly believe they exist,' I replied. 'That is why I mean to wait.'

'Violating the taboo against a returning spirit,' Chang persisted, 'is bad luck for the living. Even if the spirit of your wife does come back to you, she is no longer a human being but has already become part of the nether world of Hades. If your beloved were really here you still would not see her without her human form, and you might risk arousing her powers of evil.'

At the moment, I could not control the madness of love in my heart.

'Life and death are pre-ordained,' I cried wildly. 'If you are so concerned for my safety, why don't you keep me company yourself?'

'For your protection, I shall stay right outside the door,' Chang replied. 'If you see anything strange, call me and I shall come in.'

Taking up a lamp, I went into Yuen's room, where everything seemed as it always had, except that the voice and face of my love were no longer there. Unable to help it, I broke into a flood of heart-broken tears.

Then, afraid that my sight might be blurred and I would miss what I so longed to see, I stopped crying and with wide-open eyes sat down on the bed to wait. Picking up my beloved's discarded dress which lay beside me, I held it in my arms and started stroking it. The cloth still held in its folds the fragrance of her body and I soon became so overcome with emotion that I lost consciousness for a moment.

'How could I have let myself fall asleep when I was waiting for her spirit to return!' I thought as I became aware of my surroundings again. Opening my eyes, I looked into all four corners of the room. I saw the two candles burning brightly on the table; but, even as I looked at them, their flames began shrinking slowly until they were no larger than beans.

I was horror-struck. My hair stood on end and my whole body was seized with an icy shiver. To stop my trembling, I rubbed my hands together and wiped my forehead, staring steadily at the candles all the time. Suddenly, both candle flames commenced to rise until they were more than a foot high and in danger of setting fire to the paper ceiling, and the light had become so bright that the whole room was lit up. Then, just as suddenly, the flames began shrinking and growing dimmer, until they were as tiny as before.

By this time my heart was pounding and my legs trembling. I wanted to call Chang to come in and look, but remembering Yuen's gentle spirit and retiring nature, I changed my mind, afraid that the presence in the room of a living stranger might distress her. Instead, I began calling her name, and implored her to appear to me. But nothing happened. I remained alone in the silence and dimness. Finally the candle flames became bright again, but did not rise high as before. Then I went out and told Yu-men what I had seen. He thought me very strong and fearless, not knowing that mine was only the strength and bravery of love.

After Yuen's death I remembered the poet Lin Ho-ching of whom it was said he took a plum tree for wife and a stork for son, and decided to take as my intimate name Mei-i, 'One who has lost his Plum Tree'. For the time being, I buried Yuen at Yang-chow, following her last wish. I bought space for her coffin at a spot called the Precious Pagoda of the Ho Family, outside the West Gate, on Golden Cassia Hill. Then I took her ancestral tablet home with me. My mother was grief-stricken. Ch'ing-chun and Feng-shen, when they came home, both wept bitterly and put on mourning clothes.

'Father is still angry and has not yet forgiven you,' Ch'i-t'ang told me at once. 'I advise you to go back to Yang-chow, Brother, and stay there until Father comes home. Then I shall do my best to persuade him to relent and will send you a special letter telling you to return.'

I paid my respects to my mother and said good-bye to my children, crying bitterly all the time; then I went back to Yang-chow. I earned my living there by selling paintings, but managed to spend most of my time mourning at Yuen's grave; forlorn and solitary; 'one body—one shadow'; sunk in abject misery, utter loneliness, and despair. The sight of our old home, whenever I had to pass it, was more than my heart could bear.

By the time the festival of Mounting the Heights arrived, on the ninth day of the ninth month, the surrounding graves had all turned yellow, but Yuen's mound was still green.

'This is a lucky site for a grave,' said the grave-keeper. 'The forces of earth must be very strong here.'

Wordlessly, I prayed to Yuen: 'The autumn wind is blowing and I am still wearing an unlined gown. If you have any super-natural powers, beloved, help me to get a job to support my-self for the rest of the year, while I am waiting here for news from home.'

Not long afterwards, Mr. Chang Yu-an, a secretary at the Chiang-tu (Yang-chow) yamen, wishing to return home to Chekiang to bury his parents, asked me to be his substitute for three months, which took care of me through the winter. At the same time, Chang Yu-men invited me to live in his home while I had the temporary appointment. Chang had lost his job also, and as he was having difficulty settling his debts at the year's end, I emptied my pockets of what money I had left, about twenty dollars, and lent it to him.

'This is the money I have saved to take my dead wife's body home for burial,' I told him. 'When I get word to go home, you can repay me.'

I stayed in Chang's home for the rest of the year, then passed the New Year there. From daybreak to dark, I did nothing but wonder what was happening at home but no word came from Ch'i-t'ang. In the third month of that year, the year of the rat, 1804, Ch'ing-chun wrote to tell me that my father was ill. I wanted to go back to Soochow immediately but was afraid that I might arouse all the old anger and bitterness. While I was hesitating, deciding first on one thing, then on another, I received a second letter from my daughter with the sad news that my father had already left this world. An intolerable pain pierced my bones and with an aching heart I cried aloud to an unheeding Heaven!

Without a moment's delay I rushed home through a starry night. Wailing loudly, I knocked my head against my father's coffin until the blood flowed. Alas! Alas! My father's whole life was one of sorrow and hardship. He spent it in hurrying from place to place, always working far from home. He had produced, in me, a worthless and degenerate son, who gave him no pleasure in his lifetime and was not present to take care of him in his last illness. Never can I escape the consequences of my unfilial conduct!

Seeing that I wept so bitterly, my mother asked me why I had not come home earlier.

'That I came home at all, is due only to the fact that your grand-child Ch'ing-chun wrote to me,' I told her.

My mother looked at my brother's wife, who had not a word to say.

I went behind the curtain to keep watch beside the coffin again. During the entire seven weeks of mourning no one spoke to me of family matters nor was I included in any of the discussions of funeral arrangements. But as I too blamed myself for not having fulfilled my duties as a son, I had no face to question them.

One day some men arrived unexpectedly to see me, demanding repayment of a loan. They came pushing through the gate, talking loudly and making a lot of noise. I went out to speak to them.

'You are within your rights to demand repayment of the debt,' I agreed, 'but my father's flesh and bones are not yet cold. Have you no respect for my sorrow that you take advantage of this moment to make such an indecent outcry?'

One of the men in the group took me aside.

'We were sent here by someone on purpose to cause this commotion,' he told me. 'But if you will stay out of sight, sir, I will go directly to the man who hired us and demand the money from him.'

'I owe the money, and I shall repay it,' I answered. 'Now get out of here at once, all of you.'

Promptly and respectfully, the men left. Then I sent for Ch'i-t'ang to come in.

'I may have been a bad son,' I said to him, 'but I have never done anything really wrong. If you believe I intend to claim any part of the family property, remember that in the past I have not received a single thing. I came home only to attend the funeral—to behave as a son to his father. How could you think that I came to argue and fight over possessions?

'An honourable man should depend upon himself alone. Since I came home with nothing, I shall leave with nothing!'

Afterwards, I went behind the curtain again, where I could mourn unseen. Then I went to say good-bye to my mother before going to see Ch'ing-chun to tell her that like Chang Liang of old, who renounced the world to follow the Red Pine Master, I was going to the mountains to become a wandering Taoist monk. While my daughter was doing her best to dissuade me, she was interrupted by the arrival of two of my friends, who had been looking for me. They were the Hsia brothers; Nan-hsün, with the literary name of Tan-an,

Tranquillity; and Feng-t'ai, whose literary name was I-shan, Clustering Peaks. The Hsias now added their opposing voices to Ch'ing-chun's, pleading with me not to go, arguing:

'It is only natural, with a family like yours, that you should feel angry and indignant. But though your father is dead, your mother is still alive. You have lost your wife but your son still needs your help. If you actually renounce the world under these circumstances, do you think you will find peace of heart?'

'What else is there for me to do?' I asked.

'Do us the honour to stay at our home for the present,' Tan-an said. 'I hear that your friend the prefect Shih Ch'o-t'ang is coming home soon on leave of absence. Why not wait until he gets here and go to see him? He will certainly be able to find something for you.'

'Unfortunately, the hundred days of mourning for my father are not over yet,' I answered. 'As you and your brother have your parents at home, I feel that my coming would be unsuitable and inconvenient.'

'But it is my father's wish also,' I-shan said. 'He joins us in extending the invitation. However, if you still think it would not be proper, I have another suggestion. There is a Buddhist temple to the west of our house where the abbot is a good friend of mine. If he could find a bed for you there, would that be all right?'

I told him I liked the idea very much. Then Ch'ing-chun said to me: 'The property Grandfather left is worth not less than three or four thousand gold pieces. I know you have refused to accept the smallest part of it, but you must at least take your travelling bag with you when you go. I can get it and bring it to the temple myself, if you will allow me.'

In this way I received not only my bag but a number of things belonging to my father, paintings, books, ink-stones and brush-pots, which Ch'ing-chun had thoughtfully packed inside it.

At the temple, a monk arranged for me to stay in the Pavilion of Great Compassion. The building faced south and near it, on the east, stood an image of the Buddha. I set up my bed in a western room of the pavilion, one which was used as a dining-room by pilgrims to the temple. One wall of this room had a moon widow exactly opposite the Buddha and, standing at the door, very fierce-looking and awe-inspiring, a figure of Kuan Sheng, the war god, brandishing a knife in his hand. From the middle of the courtyard a silver gingko tree, with a trunk three men could not have encircled with their arms, threw its shade over the entire pavilion.

In the stillness of the night the wind roared like a wild animal and my friend I-shan, who often came with fruit and wine to keep me company, asked: 'Staying here all alone, aren't you afraid when you wake up in the middle of the night?'

'I have always lived an honest life,' I answered. 'I have no memories of wrong-doing to disturb my heart. Why should I be afraid?'

A short time after my arrival at the temple, it began to rain, a heavy downpour that continued without a break, night and day, for more than thirty days. I became concerned about the gingko tree, afraid that one of the boughs might break, crush the roof beams and collapse the pavilion. But, thanks to the protection of the gods, nothing happened. Outside the temple however, walls collapsed, houses without number fell into ruins and the surrounding fields of rice and grain were completely flooded. But I spent the whole time with the monks, painting all day long, and saw and heard nothing.

At the beginning of the seventh month the skies began to clear, and when I-shan's father left for Ch'ung-ming on business I went with him as his secretary, for which he paid me twenty gold pieces. When I returned, my father's grave was being prepared. Ch'i-t'ang sent my son Feng-shen to me with a message.

'Younger Brother is short of money on account of all the funeral expenses,' he told the boy to say. 'Will you give him ten or twenty gold pieces?' I was emptying my pockets to give him all I had but I-shan stopped me, insisting on giving half the amount himself. Then I took Ch'ing-chun with me and went on ahead to my father's burial place. After the funeral, I returned again to the Pavilion of Great Compassion.

At the end of the ninth month I-shan, who had some property at Yung-t'ai Sands in Tung-hai, took me with him when he went there to collect his share of the profits, and for the next two months we idled about, relaxing, and enjoying ourselves. When we arrived home again, winter was drawing to a close. Moving to I-shan's home, I stayed with him until after the New Year, in a studio called the Snow and Wild Goose Grass Hut.

How different was my friend's behaviour from that of my own flesh and blood!

In the seventh month of the year of the ox, 1805, Shih Ch'o-t'ang returned home from Peking. Ch'o-t'ang was his intimate name, his given name being Yün-yu and his literary name, Chih-ju. We had been friends from early childhood.

After winning first place in the Imperial Examinations under the Emperor Ch'ien-lung, in the year of the dog, 1790, Ch'o-t'ang went to Sze-chuan as prefect of Chung-king. During the uprising of the White Lotus Sect he spent three years in the cavalry, becoming famous for his bravery in fighting the rebels. When he came home we were delighted to see each other and later, on the Double Ninth Festival, the ninth day of the ninth month, when he was leaving with his family for Chung-king again, he asked me to go with him.

I went to kow-tow and take leave of my mother, who was staying at the home of Lu Shang-wu, my ninth sister's husband, as my father's house now belonged to strangers.

'You must do everything you can to add lustre to the family name,' my mother instructed me. 'Your brother can be neither depended upon nor trusted and you are my only hope. I am depending entirely on you.'

Feng-shen wanted to see me off, but before we had gone half way, he began crying uncontrollably, so that I had to send him home.

We went by boat to Ching-k'ou. Ch'o-t'ang had an old friend, Wang Ti-fu, a graduate of the second degree who was an official in the Huai-yang Salt Bureau at Yang-chow, and he was taking this round-about way in order to visit Wang. I went to Yang-chow with Ch'o-t'ang, where I was able to go and care for Yuen's grave once more. After that, the boat turned around and followed the course of the Yang-tze upstream, against the current. Enjoying all the famous scenery as we passed, we finally arrived at Ching-chou, in Hupei province, where Ch'o-t'ang received the news of his promotion to the position of tao-t'ai in Tung-kuan. Consequently, he left me behind in Ching-chou for the time being, with his son Tun-fu and his family, while he and his now diminished retinue rode off to pass the New Year at Chung-king. From there he would go on to his new office by way of Cheng-tu.

In the second month of the year of the tiger, 1806, the rest of his family set out to join him, going by way of the river only as far as Fan-ch'eng. From this point we continued our journey by land. The road was long and the expenses very great. The carts were all overloaded, heavy with people and baggage. Horses died of exhaustion and cart-wheels broke under the strain. It was truly an exhausting experience, a journey beset with hardship and trouble.

A bare three months after our arrival at Tung-kuan, Ch'o-t'ang was again promoted, this time to the office of provincial judge at Shan-tso.

My friend being an honest official, the wind blowing clear through both his sleeves, he could not afford to take his family with him. Staying behind in Tung-kuan, we lived temporarily at Tung-ch'uan College until, at the end of ten months, when he began to receive his salary at Shan-tso, Ch'o-t'ang sent a special message asking us to join him. In his letter, he enclosed a note from Ch'ing-chun telling me the shocking news that Feng-shen had died in the fourth month.

Remembering the tears he had shed as he saw me off on my journey, I realized that they had been tears of farewell. Father and son were never to meet again in this life!

Alas! Feng-shen was Yuen's only son. Could he not have been spared to father her descendants?

Ch'o-t'ang was very distressed when he heard the sad news and gave me a concubine to divert my thoughts. From that time on, my life has seemed unreal, an existence full of turmoil and trouble, a dream from which I don't know when I shall awaken.

*Printed in England
at The Curwen Press
Plaistow, E.13*